Literary Patronage in Late Medieval Japan

Michigan Papers in Japanese Studies, Number 23
Center for Japanese Studies
The University of Michigan

Literary Patronage in Late Medieval Japan

Edited by Steven D. Carter

Center for Japanese Studies
The University of Michigan
Ann Arbor, Michigan, 1993

Library of Congress Cataloging-in-Publication Data

Literary Patronage in late medieval Japan / edited by Steven D. Carter.
ix, 175p. 23cm. — (Michigan Papers in Japanese Studies ; no. 23)
Includes index.
ISBN 0-939512-60-2
1. Japanese poetry—1185–1600—History and criticism. 2. Authors and patrons—Japan—History. 3. Literary patrons—Japan—Biography. I. Carter, Steven D. II. Series.
PL733.33.P38L58 1993
895.6'1209—dc20 93–14920
CIP

The paper used in this publication meets the requirements of the ANSI Standard Z39.48-1984 (Permanence of Paper).

Printed in the United States of America

Contents

Preface

This volume of essays is the outcome of a special conference on Japanese literature, art, and culture sponsored by the Center for Japanese Studies at the University of California, Berkeley, in April 1986. The conference was organized by William H. McCullough (University of California, Berkeley), with support provided by the Graduate Division, the College of Letters and Science, the Institute of East Asian Studies, and the Center for Japanese Studies at the University of California, Berkeley, and by the Berkeley East Asian National Resource Center. The conference brought together five Japanese and four American scholars, assisted by three discussants, for the task of exploring the general theme of patrons and patronage of the arts in Japan during the late medieval period.

In addition to Professors Carter, Horton, Kaneko, Kumakura, and Tsurusaki, who have contributed articles to this volume, the scholars who presented papers to the conference included Thomas Hare, Kawai Masatomo, Oka Masahiko, and Esperanza Ramirez-Christensen. To each of these we express our thanks. Special gratitude is also due Maribeth Graybill, Chiyuki Kumakura, and Susan Matisoff, whose service as discussants added much to the success of the conference. We also wish to thank those who provided administrative assistance before, during, and after the conference, especially Eugenie T. Bruck of the Center for Japanese Studies.

For his patience and care in the editing process we thank Bruce E. Willoughby, Managing Editor of the Center for Japanese Studies at the University of Michigan.

Contributors

Steven D. Carter is Professor in the Department of East Asian Languages and Literatures at the University of California, Irvine. He has recently completed a life-study of the statesman-scholar Ichijō Kaneyoshi.

H. Mack Horton, Assistant Professor in the Department of East Asian Languages at the University of California, Berkeley, is currently working on a translation and study of the journals of Sōchō.

Kaneko Kinjirō, Emeritus Professor and former Dean of the Faculty in Literature at Hiroshima University, has also taught at Tōkai University and Nishogakusha University. Recipient of the Ministry of Education Prize and other awards, he is the author of numerous books and articles on Japanese linked verse.

Kumakura Isao is Professor at the Kokuritsu Minzokugaku Hakubutsukan in Osaka. A cultural historian, his main field of research is the tea ceremony.

Tsurusaki Hirō, currently Professor at Tezukayama Gakuin Tanki Daigaku, has published widely on subjects related to medieval Japanese poets and culture.

Introduction

Steven D. Carter

In recent years, scholars of premodern European culture have stressed the importance of understanding the dynamics of patronage in any consideration of the arts, particularly in the case of the medieval and Renaissance eras, when almost all artistic production was undertaken within the bounds of some kind of patron-client relationship.[1] It should surprise no one that in Japan, too, scholars are beginning to show more interest in the social and political contexts of artistic creation. No longer are the great works of classical and medieval civilization examined as if they existed in a formalistic vacuum: art, as other cultural commodities, is now seen more and more as arising from a particular historical and social setting, often a setting that involves tangible support from those with the means and predilection to promote their artistic interests.

In a dictionary, no word in the classical Japanese vocabulary corresponds in a precise way to English *patron* (a word derived ultimately from the Latin word *pater,* or father), which occurs as early as the fourteenth century in reference to those who stand in relation to others—particularly artists—as protectors or lords. Indeed, even

1. The landmark study of the topic is Francis Haskell, *Patrons and Painters: A Study in the Relations between Italian Art and Society in the Age of the Baroque* (New York: Alfred A. Knopf, 1963). Other essays that I have found useful in preparation for this study are contained in Guy Fitch Lytle and Stephen Orgel, eds., *Patronage in the Renaissance* (Princeton: Princeton University Press, 1981) and Michael Foss, *The Age of Patronage* (Ithaca, New York: Cornell University Press, 1971).

the modern language tends to use a loanword—*patoron*—rather than Japanese equivalents. Yet no one with any knowledge of premodern Japanese civilization can be ignorant of the important role of patronage in the production of all the traditional arts, from the more obvious cases of painting and architecture to the less well documented areas of poetry and the other literary arts.

Students of Nara and Heian culture will be well aware of the patterns of patronage during the heyday of the imperial court. Then there was really only one primary class of patrons—the court itself, which included the imperial house and the aristocratic families, as well as the noble clerics of important temples and monasteries in the capital and home provinces. It is this class and its highly refined tastes that we must thank for the architecture and sculpture of classical Japan, found almost exclusively in temples that themselves were built by emperors or high nobles; for the poetry of the imperial collections and numerous poetry contests and gatherings, so often recorded on finely decorated paper that is itself thought of as a work of art; and for the scroll paintings, portraits, decorated sutras and other Buddhist paraphernalia, fine wood furnishings, musical works and instruments, and all else that is now regarded as the heritage of classical civilization. Even literary classics such as *Genji monogatari* ("The Tale of Genji") and *Makura no sōshi* ("The Pillow Book of Sei Shōnagon") owe their existence, in part at least, to a habit of imperial and aristocratic patronage that brought the talents of ladies like Murasaki Shikibu and Sei Shōnagon, along with their contemporaries Izumi Shikibu, Akazome Emon, and Ise Tayū, to the court and then encouraged them in their artistic tendencies, if not in their specific endeavors.[2]

Although in increasingly attenuated forms, this pattern of imperial and aristocratic patronage continued into the medieval period. Thus Kujō Michiie (1193–1252), imperial regent in the mid-

2. If proof is required for such an assertion, one need only note that all the great Nara temples, which were as much centers of art as religion, were built by emperors or the great aristocractic families—Hōryūji by Shōtoku Taishi, Yakushiji and Tōdaiji by Emperor Shōmu, Kōfukuji by the Fujiwara, etc.—and the same situation pertained in and around Kyoto in later centuries. Likewise, the *hachidaishū*—the first eight imperial anthologies of *waka*—were conceived, published, and distributed with imperial and aristocratic support. Although no scroll paintings from the early or mid-Heian period have survived, records of those times make it

Kamakura period and a patron of poets and artists of all sorts, was able to undertake even so grand a project as the construction of the Zen temple Tōfukuji well after the high point of his family's hegemony in the late Heian period. Even as late as the 1400s an emperor like Go-Komatsu (1377–1433) had the resources necessary to sponsor a lively salon for his princely relatives, noble friends, and poets and artists from all ranks. But already in the Kamakura period there were other classes of patrons rivaling the old families, who were by then bereft of political power and ready cash. These were the great military families of the new shogunate, the Minamoto and their supporters in Kyoto and Kamakura. It was to such new and more wealthy sources of patronage rather than to the traditional aristocracy that the Zen sect looked for its primary support, and the same was true of many poets and artists astute enough to sense the desire of warriors for the kind of legitimizing power that came with participation in higher culture.

It can be argued, however, that the Minamoto and, later, the Hōjō—who came to be the real power in shogunal affairs from early in the thirteenth century—were really aristocrats themselves whose devotion to the arts did little more than extend the old patterns of patronage into a new age. Their center of activity was still largely in the old capital; their policy of financial support for the emperor and the old families did much to assure the status quo. And certainly the greatest patrons of the Kamakura period were not so much eastern warlords as men like emperors Go-Toba (1180–1239) and Fushimi (1265–1317) and the aristocrats Kujō Yoshitsune (1169–1206) and Saionji Sanekane (1249–1322).

It was not until the Muromachi period (1336–1573), in particular the late fifteenth and early sixteen centuries, which were dominated by social upheavals and political conflicts, that the most fundamental expansion of patronage took place. As any number of recent historical studies has shown, this was a time of great change in all areas of Japanese life: old centralized political establishments were giving way to new provincial powers, the growth of urban centers was causing changes in trade patterns and financial institutions, and

apparent that the court and its families were directly responsible for the major works of the day. Later classics in the genre, such as *Genji monogatari emaki* and *Ban dainagon ekotoba,* were produced at the court by court-employed artists.

everywhere the economy was creating new centers of wealth and influence.[3] In such an age of vitality all patterns of production and consumption were affected, including those involving the arts.

But how and under what specific conditions did these changes take place? The papers in this volume represent an attempt to answer that question and others like it. The historical figures focused upon range from members of the imperial family and the houses of the regency to tea masters, painters, merchants, provincial daimyo, and especially *renga* ("linked-verse") poets, whose central place in many of the papers speaks for their prominent place in medieval artistic history. But all share a common concern with patron-client relations in what many consider to be the most significant watershed in Japanese history. Because the problems dealt with are complex ones involving many levels and kinds of patronage, the essays perhaps pose more questions than they answer (To what extent were "professional" artists in these days truly "free agents"? Where does patronage end and employment begin? What effect did patron-client relations have on the works of art themselves?), but at the very least they serve the purpose of opening up a new arena of research that is essential to a full understanding of the arts in the late medieval age. In this respect they may best be understood as case studies, presented in the anticipation of further work in a long-overlooked area of cultural history.

Until very recently, men such as Asakura Takakage (1428–81) and Ōuchi Masahiro (1446–95) received scant attention from scholars of medieval Japanese art and literature, and then primarily as amateur poets whose chief significance was thought to be found in accounts of government, politics, and warfare. Many surveys of art history failed even to include their names. Now, however, cultural historians are beginning to realize that these men and the great clans they represent were powerful not only in the council chambers and on the battlefield, but also in the salons, studies, studios, and theater halls of their age. For it was such military men—a phrase to be

3. See, for instance, John Whitney Hall and Toyoda Takeshi, eds., *Japan in the Muromachi Age* (Berkeley: University of California Press, 1977) and George Elison and Bardwell L. Smith, eds., *Warlords, Artists, & Commoners: Japan in the Sixteenth Century* (Honolulu: University Press of Hawaii, 1981).

understood here in the broad sense of those of military upbringing and affiliation—who were some of the foremost patrons of the traditional arts in an age of transition when the products of the court heritage were being carried to an expanding audience whose aristocratic artistic tastes were acquired through study and connoisseurship rather than birth.

The most famous of these warrior patrons were of course the Ashikaga shoguns, who from their palaces in Kyoto sponsored much of the cultural life of that city for a period of nearly two hundred years. Even Takauji (1305–58), roughest and most soldierly of the Ashikaga line, was an avid poet who lent his support to the Nijō family of poets and was instrumental in the commissioning of the eighteenth imperial *waka* collection, *Shin senzaishū* ("New Collection of a Thousand Years," 1359). And his heirs—all fourteen of them, but especially Yoshimitsu (1358–1408), Yoshinori (1394–1441), Yoshimasa (1436–90), and Yoshihisa (1465–89)—carried on his tradition of involvement with the arts. All of the last three imperial collections of *waka* were to a large extent products of Ashikaga goodwill.

Some Ashikaga patronage came in the form of institutionalized support, often carried out by official "commissioners" (*bugyō*) who received stipends for their labors. This was the case, for instance, in the world of *renga,* which from the early fifteenth century onward enjoyed sponsorship by the shogunate through the Kitano Shrine Linked-Verse Laureate (*sōshō*), an appointee of the government.[4] But it was by way of the personal patronage of the various shoguns themselves that the arts received their greatest support. Each of these generally had his own staff of *dōbōshū*—a term that literally means something like "colleague" or "companion"—who acted as collectors of paintings, pottery, and other decorative pieces, curators of their master's artifacts, arbiters of taste, and general artistic jacks-of-all-trades. With such men surrounding them, the shoguns filled their calendars with all forms of art and entertainment, beginning with the aristocratic arts of *uta* poetry and extending on to more contemporary amusements such as linked-verse parties, recitations by *biwa* minstrels, tea gatherings and competitions, and performances of dance,

4. Strictly speaking, the shogunal appointment and the Kitano Shrine appointment were separate until well into the sixteenth century, although often the same person held both posts.

sarugaku, and *kyōgen* companies. Finally, the shoguns built themselves grand residences and retreats as places to house their artifacts, pursue their cultural interests, and greet their many guests, in the process creating fine works of architecture like Kinkakuji, Yoshimitsu's "Golden Pavilion," and Ginkakuji, Yoshimasa's "Silver Pavilion," which were surrounded by beautiful landscape and walking gardens and decorated within by paintings commissioned from artists such as Kanō Masanobu (ca. 1434–ca. 1530).[5]

Sharing the habit of artistic patronage with the shogunal house were other great military families of the time—the Shiba, the Hosokawa, the Hatakeyama, and the Yamana from the beginning, and later on the Ōuchi and other *tozama* lords ("outside" families not connected to the Ashikaga by blood or longtime feudal ties). These too had their own *dōbōshū* and sponsored their own entertainments and cultural projects, as well as supporting the Ashikaga in their endeavors. There were many reasons for this, a prominent one being that the warrior elite was anxious to identify themselves with traditional sources of authority and prestige, the aristocratic families and their artistic life-styles.[6] But an early strategy of the shogunate that eventually coerced or lured most of the great *shugo daimyō* houses into maintaining a residence in the capital must also be given credit for the expansion of artistic patronage at this time.[7] In the capital, the Ashikaga were able to require various acts of fealty of their vassals, thus making firm the feudal ties that were their surest source of power. One by-product of life in the capital was increased exposure to the arts of the sort seldom experienced fully in the provinces.

5. For a study of shogunal patronage in the era of Yoshimitsu, see H. Paul Varley, "Ashikaga Yoshimitsu and the World of Kitayama: Social Change and Shogunal Patronage in Early Medieval Japan," in Hall and Toyoda. See also Kenneth Alan Grossberg, *Japan's Renaissance: The Politics of the Muromachi Bakufu* (Cambridge: Harvard University Press, 1981), 30–38.
6. See Grossberg, *Japan's Renaissance,* 30.
7. Utsunomiya ties with the Nijō family were particularly strong, the foundation of their association being the marriage of Fujiwara Tameie (1198–1275), son and heir of Teika (1162–1241), to an Utsunomiya woman in the mid-1200s. Tameie's son, Tameuji (1222–86), and later heirs of the Nijō house maintained a close relationship with the Utsunomiya family for generations to come. For more information see Tonomura Nobuko, *Kamakura no kajin* (Kamakura: Shunjusha, 1986).

Ironically, however, it was less this increased presence of the *shugo daimyō* in the capital that had profound implications for the arts than the return of those same *shugo daimyō* to their estates in the countryside. For when the warrior chieftains and their captains went home, they took the culture of the capital with them. It was this fact more than any other that led to the much-changed profile of artistic patronage in late Muromachi Japan.

Undoubtedly, this trend had begun long before. As students of *Man'yōshū* ("Collection of Ten Thousand Leaves," ca. 759) know, there was a considerable artistic community in northern Kyushu even in the eighth century. Moreover, provincial families such as the Utsunomiya, whose main estates were in the East Country near Kamakura, were involved in producing their own anthologies of court poetry in the 1200s,[8] and one can cite many other instances of cultural interest in the provinces, some going back to the Heian period. The greatest movement in this direction, however, clearly came much later, in the fifteenth century, particularly during and after the Ōnin War of 1467–77, a conflict that did much to destroy the capital and sent both warriors and some of the aristocracy into the provinces for safety.

One family that presents itself as an outstanding example of this trend is the Ōuchi, a *tozama* clan that had its base of support in the provinces of western Honshu. Coming originally from the *kokujin* class of local landholders, the clan had risen to *shugo* status, although not without Ashikaga resistance, in the mid-fourteenth century. Thereafter they were by turns allies and enemies of the shogunate in a series of national, regional, and local conflicts. By the time of Ōuchi Yoshihiro (1356–99), the family was in control of seven western provinces, presenting the shogunate with one of its most difficult political challenges.

Yoshihiro, who died in an uprising against the central government, was himself a man not unacquainted with the courtly arts, especially linked verse, which he studied under the instruction of the courtier-scholar Nijō Yoshimoto (1320–88).[9] But his long campaigns left him little time to pursue artistic interests. His heir,

8. See Yonehara Masayoshi, *Sengoku bushi to bungei no kenkyū* (Tokyo: Ōfūsha, 1976), 517–22.
9. Ibid., 534–54.

Morimi (1377–1431), on the other hand, maintained a residence in the capital continuously after his succession as Ōuchi chieftain in 1399, during which time he was one of the foremost politicians of the central government and, not surprisingly, an active participant in artistic life. As Yonehara Masayoshi has shown in his monumental study *Sengoku bushi to bungei no kenkyū* ("Essays on the Warriors of the Warring States Period and the Arts"), Zen monks were frequent visitors at Morimi's Kyoto home, where he sponsored poetry meetings in a special pavilion designed for that and other leisure pursuits. Nor was he only an onlooker in literary events: true to a pattern that will be seen to characterize many other warrior-patrons, he was an amateur artist himself. He even studied *uta* composition under the renowned poet-scholar Kazan'in Nagachika (1345?–1429), leaving to posterity a collection of his poetry.[10]

The Ouchi involvement in artistic patronage and participation was therefore already firmly established in the times of the shoguns Yoshimitsu and Yoshinori. Mochiyo (1394–1441), Morimi's heir, continued the tradition, living to see three of his poems actually included in an imperial *waka* collection before meeting his end at a *sarugaku* performance along with the shogun Ashikaga Yoshinori.[11] But it was Mochiyo's grandson Masahiro who became the most famous of all the scions of the Ōuchi clan, as well as its greatest patron of the arts. Although born and raised in Yamaguchi, provincial seat and stronghold of Suō, Masahiro seems to have had a classical education, emphasizing poetry in particular. And while in the capital as one of the primary generals of the western army during the Ōnin War, he continued his devotion to the arts as time allowed during interruptions in the fighting.

In December of 1477, Masahiro led his troops out of the capital—made a ruin by ten years of warfare in its streets—toward home, where he lived for twenty more years as one of the few *shugo daimyō* able to retain his power in the decades to come. His stronghold at Yamaguchi became one of the burgeoning "little Kyotos" of that time, serving not only as a congregating place for his vassals and a place of residence for local artists, but also as a stop for *sarugaku* troupes,

10. Yoshinori was assassinated in the summer of 1441 by Akamatsu Mitsuhide in a short skirmish referred to as the Kakitsu Disturbance.

11. Ibid., 579–640.

renga poets, and painters. Historical records show that Masahiro had extensive contacts with almost all of the cultural figures of his time, including the aristocratic scholars Ichijō Kaneyoshi (1402–81) and Sanjōnishi Sanetaka (1455–1537), the courtly *waka* poet Asukai Masachika (1416–90), the *sarugaku* writer-performer Konparu Zenchiku (b. 1403?), the *renga* masters Iio Sōgi (1421–1502) and Kensai (1452–1510), and the monk-painter Sesshū (1420–1506). Many of these, especially the *renga* poets and Sesshū, stayed for long periods in Masahiro's domains, where they practiced their arts and acted as teachers to local devotees, under Masahiro's protection and often at his expense. And, as if this were not enough to show his commitment, he also did much to sponsor events back in the capital, such as the compilation of the *Shinsen tsukubashū* ("New Tsukuba Collection," 1495), second of the imperially recognized collections of linked verse. The extent of Masahiro's endeavors as a collector of artifacts and manuscripts alone shows that for him the traditional arts were not mere adornments but a way of life. *Ise monogatari* ("Tales of Ise"), *Genji monogatari,* the imperial *waka* collections, and commentaries on the same were all contained in his library, some of them brought back from the capital at the end of the war, but many others solicited from courtiers and scholars in a lively correspondence that continued until his death.[12]

One of the most prominent of these correspondents was in fact later to become a kind of courtier-in-residence in Yamaguchi. His name was Sanjō Kimiatsu (d. 1507), and he was a high-ranking noble in every respect: a member of the Kan'in branch of the Fujiwara belonging to the *seigake* lineage, whose heirs could rise to the position of chancellor (*daijō daijin*) in the court hierarchy. As was the case with many other nobles of the time, however, his high titles meant little after the Ōnin War. His story is nothing unusual, then, but it serves as well as any other to provide a paradigm for the fate of his class in the declining days of court power.

Kimiatsu's life began in Kyoto, where he lived among the mansions of the nobility. His father rose to the rank of Minister of the Left, and Kimiatsu too climbed the official ladder at the expected pace, becoming a Major Counselor in 1458, Palace Minister in 1476, and Minister of the Right in 1479. Even before he could officially

12. Ibid., 585–95, 600–8.

celebrate this last appointment, however, circumstances sent him away from the capital. As one diarist put the matter, "Since the disturbance, revenues from the family estates have scattered in all directions, with no return to stability as yet. Life in Kyoto has become simply intolerable for him."[13] The "disturbance" of course refers to the Ōnin War, which affected the economic situation of most noble houses in a way summed up by the words of another courtier, Nakamikado Nobutane (d. 1525), who opined that Kimiatsu had been motivated to leave the capital "because of poverty."[14] At the time, Kimiatsu's father was himself living in poverty in a rented house. Sanjōnishi Sanetaka and other noble friends gathered to bid Kimiatsu farewell but were too destitute themselves to offer more practical help.

The place he chose for his new home was called Fukagawa, in the Ōuchi domains near Nagato. The reasons for the choice are simple: there were family estates there and perhaps even relatives, since an earlier Ōuchi lord appears to have taken a Sanjō woman to wife. His coming, then, was probably not unexpected; it may even have been welcomed, as his talents as a poet and scholar would prove useful to the literary-minded Masahiro. Not long after his arrival in Fukagawa, Kimiatsu resigned his offices at court and took the tonsure as a lay monk. Thereafter, for the nearly three decades until his death in 1507, he lived in the Ōuchi domains, with only one short sojourn away in 1486. In effect, he was to the Ōuchi chieftain a teacher who instructed his patron in both *uta* and *renga,* as well as a curator who helped collect and copy manuscripts for Masahiro's library, which included not only court classics, but the Confucian classics, Buddhist sutras, and works of history, medicine, and traditional lore. Kimiatsu himself maintained some contact with friends and relatives in the capital, sometimes using Sōgi and other traveling artists as couriers. But, in all, his concerns for these last years of his life centered primarily in Fukagawa.

Until the Ōuchi clan came to its end in the mid-sixteenth century, artists and scholars of all sorts continued to find patrons in Yamaguchi and other places under Ōuchi control. And there were a

13. From *Nagaoki Sukune ki.* Quoted in Yonehara, *Sengoku bushi to bungei no kenkyū,* 600.

14. From *Nobutanekyōki.* Quoted in Yonehara, *Sengoku bushi to bungei no kenkyū,* 600.

number of other such "little Kyotos" as well—one at Ichijōdani in Echizen, stronghold of the Asakura; another in Noto, seat of the Hatakeyama; and still others in Wakasa, Ise, Suruga, Musashi, and northern Kyushu.[15] Indeed, one can go so far as to say that for the next hundred years or so, Kyoto ceased to totally dominate the artistic landscape of the country as it had done for so many centuries before. The picture Yonehara's study paints is one of real diversity, with a number of daimyo competing against each other in a variety of ways, not the least being in acts of patronage. Usually the model is the same: a strong man of artistic interests at the head of a clan, surrounding himself with vassals of similar propensities and sponsoring a variety of activities. Some daimyo had their own *renga* masters, as in the case of Sōchō (1448–1532), whose long service to the Imagawa family is analyzed in Mack Horton's essay; others sponsored their own *sarugaku* performers; and not a few were substantial poets, calligraphers, and painters in their own right, in whom the artists of the time found avid and wealthy students. Virtually all of them supported the arts—meaning everything from traditional poetry to music, court kickball (*kemari*), dance, and tea—in one way or another as part of the obligations entailed in their high positions on the social ladder. Their domains came to form a circuit traveled by peripatetic artists of all sorts, even including aristocrats like Sanjō Kimiatsu who were no longer able to make a life for themselves in the capital. Nor did this outward-moving trend cease any time soon; indeed, as time went on such artistic activity in the provinces increased, continuing on beyond the Tokugawa peace of 1600 and changing the contours of elite patronage and elite culture for all generations to come.

Meanwhile, patterns of patronage back in the capital were changing too. As Kaneko Kinjirō's paper makes clear, the imperial family was still very much involved in patronage, perhaps even more so than in those past ages when it had been compelled to divide its time more equally among ceremonial, political, and artistic activities. But the resources of the emperors, retired emperors, and their princes, princesses, and ladies were clearly not as substantial as they had been

15. In his study, Yonehara treats the artistic activities of the Hatakeyama, Asakura, Takeda, Ōuchi, and Imagawa clans during the Muromachi and Warring States periods. Also of note are the Uesugi in Echigo and the Kantō, the Kitabatake in Ise, the Saitō in Mino, as well as a host of other smaller clans too numerous to mention.

in earlier eras. Now they could afford to offer their support to projects only with the assistance of outside money, usually coming from the shogunate or other military families. Thus it is that the curious phenomena of "multilayered" patronage is encountered, in which an Ōuchi Masahiro provides backing to an imperial project (such as the compilation of *Shinsen tsukubashū*) that is in turn turned over to an aristocrat (Sanjōnishi Sanetaka) and several professional poets (Sōgi, most prominently) who perform the actual work (of study, sorting, collation, and so forth). It is precisely such overlappings in the design of late Muromachi patronage that make precise definitions so difficult to formulate.

If this was true for the imperial house, it was even more true for the old aristocratic families. In my own paper, I have tried to show that Ichijō Kaneyoshi lived most of his life as a prominent patron, although one restrained by limited financial resources. It is clear, however, that by the end of his life he was also the beneficiary of support from a number of sources, including the shogunate and other military families. In his last years, he came perilously close to being a professional scholar, whose pedigree gave him and his writings prestige but little financial security, and certainly not the resources to undertake the kinds of patronage routinely indulged in by his ancestors.

The life of Sanjōnishi Sanetaka is another case in point. Born fifty years after Kaneyoshi and into a family of lesser rank in the official hierarchy, Sanetaka knew the opulence of court life in earlier ages only through books. And Kumakura Isao's essay shows that it was partly through books—or handwritten manuscripts, more precisely—rather than through traditional sources of income such as estate revenues that he made his living. For him copies of *Genji monogatari* or treatises by Fujiwara Teika were not only treasured cultural artifacts but commodities; if not a bookseller, he was at the very least a booklender whose services did not come free. Was he then not a patron in any sense? The answer of course depends on one's definition. In purely financial terms, he was not patron but patronized. But so narrow a definition does not suffice for late Muromachi Japan because in his relations with *renga* poets and even some warriors, Sanetaka was clearly considered a cultural superior of some importance, whose favor was a thing to be desired. Reputation is hard to quantify and may seem to confuse the issue, but without it one cannot understand the true patterns of patronage in Sanetaka's day.

With the other major patron classes of the late fifteenth and early sixteenth centuries, priests and merchants, one encounters another problem of definition. Looking beyond the surface, one finds that priests, warriors, merchants, and aristocrats were not always discrete groups, but overlapping classifications. Any student of the age must know, for instance, of the importance of a temple like Kōfukuji in the arts of the old capital at Nara. *Daijō-in jisha zōjiki* ("Affairs of the Temples and Shrines of the Daijō-in"), the diary of one of the *monzeki* ("cloister" or "supervisory temple") of that institution, is full of references to *renga* meetings and *sarugaku* performances.[16] But should such patronage be credited to the temple itself or to its abbots, who were nearly all the younger sons of aristocrats or shogunal families back in the capital? Aristocratic influence in the arts, even after the Ōnin War, was more extensive than people generally realize. Venerable temples such as Enryakuji and Miidera and Shinto shrines such as those as Ise, Sumiyoshi, and Kasuga were still important and powerful institutions in the late fifteenth and early sixteenth centuries—institutions whose bloodlines and tastes were inextricably linked with the old families in Kyoto. Even the great Zen temples, which are generally regarded as major enclaves of the "new" cultural currents of the Muromachi age, especially Chinese poetry, painting, and scholarship, were also well connected to the traditional aristocracy and the shogunal house and its offshoots. Once again, attempts at reducing the patronage of the age to simple divisions fail to reflect the reality of the times. A Zen monk was of course a monk first of all, with duties that made him a member of a particular establishment and class. Yet the fact cannot be ignored that he was often also an Ashikaga or a Hosokawa or an Ichijō as well. Only the lowest orders of the religious world—priests of the Time sect, and so forth—can be said to have represented the "common man" in the arts of the time, and then more as beneficiaries than as patrons.

The situation with the merchant class would seem to be simpler, but only on the surface. Tsurusaki Hirō's description of the activities of the *uta* poet Shōkō (1412–93) in Sakai supports the contention of other scholars that by the time in question there definitely was a nascent merchant class, comprising large populations in the capital, provincial daimyo strongholds, temple towns, post towns, and ports

16. See Suzuki Ryōichi, *Daijō-in jisha zōjiki: Aru monbatsu sōryo no botsuraku no kiroku* (Tokyo: Soshiete, 1983), 118–46.

such as Sakai itself and Hakata.[17] Yet it is also clear that even the traders of port cities—the most independent merchants of the day—were generally characterized by strong bonds of political and economic patronage with specific warrior chieftains or clans.[18] Real autonomy was only to come much later. What this meant for artists was that ties with daimyo and other warrior families continued to be most crucial to their welfare, merchants being considered little more than low-ranking vassals in the feudal system.

So the patterns in question were extremely complex, as might be expected in an age of great social change. Patrons existed wherever there was wealth, and sometimes even where there was little wealth but great prestige or symbolic power. Generally speaking, patronage of those arts that have survived to reveal their affiliations was created with the support, encouragement, and participation of primarily two large groups: the traditional aristocracy, including the imperial house and the noble families (meaning both those wearing court costume and those cloaked in the robes of the priesthood); and the military families, including the Ashikaga, their branch families and vassals, the great families of the provinces, and their various support groups—from vassals to merchants and others farther down the economic ladder. Beyond this, it may only be said that the trend throughout the late medieval era was outward and downward on the social scale, including even those who would eventually be constituted as a true "merchant" class in the late Sengoku and Edo periods. What such a conception lacks in precision when applied to any particular moment in time, it compensates for in comprehensiveness.

More precise things can be said about the other end of the spectrum, the artists of the age, who by and large were becoming more and more pure "professionals" as time went on. As mentioned above, artists of earlier eras had tended to be either amateurs who, however serious about their work, owed their sustenance to official rank and title at court, or employees of official institutions. By the time of the Ōnin War, however, this state of affairs had already undergone a substantial change, first among *renga* poets. The *renga* poet Shinkei (1406–75), for instance, spent most of his life as a high

17. V. Dixon Morris, "Sakai: From Shōen to Port City," in Hall and Toyoda, and "The City of Sakai and Urban Autonomy," in Elison and Smith.
18. Morris, "The City of Sakai and Urban Autonomy," 34–35.

cleric for whom poetry was not, strictly speaking, a paying occupation. But after his move to the eastern seaboard in 1467, he was dependent on the support of various military and merchant patrons—Suzuki Nagatoshi being just one among them—for his livelihood. In this way he marked an important trend in the arts of his day, for after the Ōnin War linked verse would no longer be dominated by poets for whom artistic work was an avocation, but by professionals such as Sōgi who spent most of their lives circulating among wealthy *renga* enthusiasts in the capital and the provinces. Thus, Takayama Sōzei, a retainer of the Yamana clan, and Nōa (1397–1471), a member of the Ashikaga artistic staff, were replaced by Sōchō and Kensai. It should be added that the latter pursued their art as a religious "way" and wore the robes of the priesthood, but there can be no doubt that poetry was their true occupation. The increase in the number of patrons in the provinces now made it possible for a man to make his living from a number of different sources as a kind of free agent.

Although less obviously, this trend toward professionalism is apparent in the other arts as well. Traditional court poetry, for instance, continued to be dominated by the aristocratic families for some time after the Ōnin War. Yet even here men such as Shōkō appear at this time, and his name comes up almost as frequently as Sōgi's in accounts of artistic activity outside the capital. Although not quite as popular as linked verse among the warrior classes, the old *uta* form still had its provincial connoisseurs who were happy to welcome poets and scholars into their chambers. In painting, the tea ceremony, and drama, too, the late 1400s saw an increase in provincial patronage that allowed artists to break out of the bonds of specific vassalage and pursue their art in a broader arena. As patrons increased in number, so did professional artists, in all having a liberating effect on the artistic world as a whole.

Which brings us to an important question: After the emergence of new classes and kinds of patrons, what effect did this liberation of artistic energies have on the arts themselves? This is obviously one of the most crucial questions for the student of late medieval culture, and also one of the most difficult to answer. Here I can offer only a few ideas for consideration in future research.

In specific cases—as in those treated by Kaneko Kinjirō in this volume—the effect of the patron-client relationship on "commissioned" works or performances was probably not very different than in ages past. Much work was still carried out in a rigid context and involved patron participation and interference in degrees that varied according to the status, sophistication, and personality of both the artist and his master. When it comes to the more general effects of the expansion of patronage to new classes, however, the answer must be more complex. While it may appear that the increase in numbers of patrons had the desirable effect of giving artists relatively more freedom to pursue their own interests and proclivities, one must remember that the patrons of the late medieval age were not just passive consumers of the arts but active participants. Among other things, this meant that, in cases like those involving Sanjō Kimiatsu and Ōuchi Masahiro, the patron became a student of the artist he supported, a feature of late medieval life that makes precise definition of patronage for that period particularly difficult to accomplish. It also meant a general trend toward conventionality in the arts, as in the rules of linked verse, which made it possible for anyone with literacy to participate in a linking session with the masters of the genre. It is not by chance that *sarugaku,* the tea ceremony, and *renga* are all highly formalized art forms: conventionalization was at the heart of much artistic activity in the late medieval age.

So what the artist gained in social freedom, he often lost in bondage to convention. No longer tied to one source of support or one institution, the artist could, to a certain extent, choose his own projects. But he was still bound by genre conventions that were the very essence of his professional existence, as well as by prevailing aristocratic and military tastes to a large degree. In comparison to earlier ages, he might even be said to have had less creative control. An *uta* poet like Fujiwara Teika (1162–1241), however bound to great patrons like Emperor Go-Toba, was able to exercise his own gifts in his private chambers to a degree seldom experienced by Sōgi in the context of the *za,* or *renga* session. Purists were rare in the Muromachi age, and for good reason, since most artists did not have the economic means to pursue their art with such private devotion.

Another, closely related way in which the expansion of patronage to the military and merchant classes affected the arts themselves was in the new emphasis on "communal" artistic experience. There were no doubt many reasons, some of them sociological and some philosophical, for the preference for group activities among so many patrons of the time. One reason, however, must be that the warlords of the age, always anxious to enunciate their wealth and power in concrete, symbolic ways, saw the arts as one way of displaying their power and realizing their claims as "benevolent" rulers. The tea ceremony, linked-verse or *uta* gatherings, and *sarugaku* performances no doubt appealed to patrons for their intrinsic artistic values some of the time, but it would be naive to assume that the arts did not have more practical significance as well. Regardless of his ultimate motives, it cannot be denied that displays of "good" taste—which still seems to have meant aristocratic taste—were politically useful to a man like Ōuchi Masahiro.

This raises the final question of whether any truly worthwhile art can emerge from a world restricted on the one hand by the demands of powerful patrons and on the other by rigid conventions. Here again, the question is obviously a relative one. The most one can say is that much of the art produced during this time—whether in the architecture of the detached palaces of the capital, in the Noh dramas of Zeami and Zenchiku, or the linked verse of Sōchō and Kensai—is valued highly by art historians. Before leaving the issue, however, one may take the liberty of noting that the art of the age seems to succeed largely to the degree it fails to follow exactly the conventions that made it possible in such a broad arena. Can it be purely chance that the *wabicha* ceremony has survived artistically, while the grander gatherings of the shoguns have not? Or that, after four hundred years, the great *renga* extravaganzas at Kitano Shrine are no longer read, while the sequences composed by Sōgi and a few disciples at Minase or Arima in more relaxed surroundings have become part of college curriculums?

In the end, then, the effects of the expanding horizons of artistic patronage in the late fifteenth and early sixteenth centuries were mixed. This age barely begins a revolution in genre or sensibility that the "plebeian" arts of Saikaku, Bashō, and the *ukiyoe* painters would complete much later. What late Muromachi patterns of patronage did produce, however, was painters like Sesshū and poets like Sōgi, who are noted more for virtuosity than originality, and a host of patrons who deserve more attention for their active support of the arts in a violent age.

Ichijō Kaneyoshi and the Literary Arts

Steven D. Carter

If we know anything at all about Ichijō Kaneyoshi (also read Kanera; 1402–81), it is that he was one of the great scholars of the Muromachi period, particularly of *Genji monogatari* ("The Tale of Genji"), *Nihon shoki* ("Chronicles of Japan"), and other Japanese classics. Most modern biographical dictionaries treat him in just those terms, often grouping him with Nijō Yoshimoto (1320–88) and Sanjōnishi Sanetaka (1455–1537), men dedicated to the preservation of aristocratic culture in an age of upheaval. However, Kaneyoshi was more than a scholar. He was also a poet of some repute in all of the traditional courtly forms; a literary critic and contest judge; a connoisseur of other arts, from painting and garden design to *sarugaku*; a politician and government official; and, perhaps most importantly, heir of the Ichijō family, one of the Five Houses of the Regency (*go-sekke*). He was thus recognized by his peers as one of the foremost leaders of an elite cadre of noble clans.[1]

Kaneyoshi was born in 1402, just a decade after the unification of the southern and northern courts and during the final years of the shogun Ashikaga Yoshimitsu (1358–1408), whom Kaneyoshi's father, Tsunetsugu (1358–1418), served for most of his adult life. At that time the Ichijō family lived on a large city estate in the northern section of the capital, only a short walk from the mansion of the shogun and close also to the imperial palace and the estates of others of his class. There, under the guidance of his father and his maternal grandfather

1. The five houses, all branches of the Fujiwara family, were the Ichijō, the Nijō, the Kujō, the Konoe, and the Takatsukasa.

Higashinobōjō Hidenaga (1333–1411), who could trace his own line back to the patron-saint of letters, Sugawara Michizane (845–903), Kane-yoshi spent his younger years preparing to inherit the Ichijō fortunes, tangible and otherwise. His father's library was one of the finest of the day, containing the literary and historical classics of Japan and China, and every evidence indicates that Kaneyoshi made good use of it. Not lost on him was the lesson that scholarly learning could be of great political advantage in a world where the judgments of the present were often arrived at by reference to the records of the past.

Although after the death of his father in 1418 Kaneyoshi suffered political losses at the hands of well-connected rivals among the other regency houses, he made a respectable career for himself nonetheless, becoming Palace Minister in 1421, Minister of the Right in 1424, and Minister of the Left in 1429. Finally, in 1432, at the age of thirty-one, he was made regent and chieftain of the Fujiwara clan. His appointment lasted only a short time—about two months, in fact—but records make it clear that as former regent he was still one of the most prominent men of his day. Again from 1447 to 1453, and then once more from 1467 to 1470, he served as regent; and for the rest of his life he was at the center of court events, not only as a scholar, but also as a representative of the high nobility. He was so successful that he was able to win high posts for his relations, including abbacies at major temples for five brothers and as many sons, as well as the regency for his heirs as head of the family.

If Kaneyoshi could boast of many successes at court, however, it must be said that in financial terms those successes were not as significant as they had been in earlier times. That the old court families were not as prosperous in Kaneyoshi's age as they had been in the Heian or Kamakura periods is common knowledge. By the fifteenth century, vital wealth and power were had only by those with real military clout, meaning the shogun, his vassals, and his numerous rivals, both in the capital and in the provinces. Thus, the coffers of Kaneyoshi's family were never bursting: since the days of Sanetsune (1223–84), founder of the Ichijō line, the estate holdings of the family had been drastically reduced by the constant encroachments of stewards and provincial war barons. Of the partial rights to over fifty tax-free estates (*shōen*) at one time or another under the control of the Ichijō, the revenues of only a handful remained under Kaneyoshi's direction, several located on the outskirts of the capital and several more in distant Echizen. In addition to this, the family received some temporary remuneration while he was serving as regent, collected rent on a few family deeded parcels of land, and could look for occasional support from a number of temples, chiefly Tōfukuji, Kōmyōbuji, Manshu-in, Daijō-in, and Zuishin-in. All told, the financial situation of the family was not too secure.[2]

Yet it would be a mistake to think of Kaneyoshi or his peers as reduced to genteel poverty, at least, that is, until the very end of his life, when the Ōnin War (1467–77) brought even the high nobility close to ruin. Diaries of earlier years, such as *Manzai jugō nikki* ("The Journal of Manzai"), *Kanmon gyoki* ("Journal of Things Seen and Heard"), and *Yasutomi no ki* ("The Record of Yasutomi"), show the aristocrats of the capital engaged in the sorts of activities that their ancestors centuries before had established as the preserve of the aristocracy, namely, the arts of poetry and music. However impetuous and fickle in their tastes, the Ashikaga shoguns clearly considered themselves courtiers, and they followed the tradition of their Kamakura forbears in protecting the estate revenues of court families whenever possible. Furthermore, the shoguns and their many generals, assistants, and hangers-on also sponsored a lively cultural environment that, indirectly at least, offered the noble families various means of support. Thus, while the aristocrats of Kaneyoshi's day lived in what their forebears might have described as straitened circumstances, they were still wealthy and powerful beyond the most extravagant dreams of the common man. Their society was still very much a court society occupied with courtly activities.

Another way to put this is to say that Kaneyoshi took seriously what by his time was an old tradition among those of his class—the tradition of patronage. His ancestors had of course been grand masters of that art: men like Kujō Kanezane (1149–1207), benefactor of poets and ally of the Minamoto family in the early medieval period; Kujō Michiie (1193–1252), who was directly responsible, among other things, for the building of the Zen temple Tōfukuji; and Kaneyoshi's grandfather, Nijō Yoshimoto, whose support of *renga* and *uta* poets in the mid-fourteenth century was legendary. Kaneyoshi's financial

2. For an explanation of Kaneyoshi's finances, see Nagashima Fukutarō, *Ichijō Kanera* (Tokyo: Yoshikawa Kobundan, 1959), 179–93.

situation would not allow him such ostentatious forms of benevolence. In fact, it could be argued that he was dependent upon religious establishments for his own support, in the form of livings for his many children. But still he was one of his age's greatest patrons, particularly when it came to the literary arts.

To list all of Kaneyoshi's acts of patronage would be a laborious task, for his whole life was structured around support—sometimes expressed in money, but usually in more subtle ways—for the traditional arts. One way to approach the topic, however, is to review the documents he left behind that suggest rather directly the scope of his activities as a benefactor of poets. For while Kaneyoshi has attained wide repute as a prolific author of scholarly works, it is less widely known that his name was attached to many of the most important creative efforts of his time as a writer of prefaces (*jo*), those short statements of introduction without which no medieval work seemed complete.

Although Kaneyoshi's reputation as a scholar seems to have been established early in life, there is little evidence of his belletristic work before the early spring of 1333, the time of a famous ten-thousand-verse linked-verse session held at the Kitano Shrine.[3] This meeting, which is conventionally seen as the beginning of a revival in linked verse, was actually sponsored by Ashikaga Yoshinori (1394–1441), the current shogun and one of the few men with the financial resources to conduct such a large cultural event, which involved hosting banquets, lodging participants (nearly four hundred for the 1433 event) and providing gifts. From early in his tenure as shogun Yoshinori had shown an interest in linked verse, and there was no better method of displaying that interest than with a grand spectacle at the Kitano Shrine, one of the favored institutions of the Ashikaga family. The nobility, needless to say, were happy to support him in his designs.

Besides his own entourage, which included the current regent Nijō Mochimoto (1390–1445), the abbot Manzai (1378–1435) of the Sanbō-in cloister, and a number of his own vassals, Yoshinori invited two former regents to his *renga* party: Kujō Mitsusuke and Kaneyoshi.

3. *Kitano-sha ichimanku gohokku, waki, daisan, shidai, narabi ni jō. Renga I*, vol.18 of *Katsura-no-miya-bon sōshō* (Tenri City: Yōtokusha, 1968), 315–46.

In all, twenty such major figures—including representatives of the aristocratic families, clerics, and Yoshinori's military friends—were appointed to direct twenty *za*, or composition stations. Also asked to participate were all the major semiprofessional *renga* poets of the day: the future *sōshō* ("laureate") Shōyū (fl.1430–40), Nibukawa Shin'ei (fl.1420–30), one of the shogun's favorites, and a group of men who later were to be looked back upon as the finest talents of that generation (Ninzei [fl.1440–55], Sōzei [d.1455], Chiun [d.1448], Nōa [1397–1471], and Renkai, who is known to us now by his later name of Shinkei [1406–75]).

The group for which Kaneyoshi served as leader—located in the Lotus Hall of the shrine precincts—was not the most illustrious: a few bishops, some low-ranking courtiers, and his brother-in-law, Nakamikado Toshisuke (d. 1439), a Major Counselor. But like the rest they composed their five-hundred-verse sequences during the space of a single day, handing their work in to scribes whose task it was to prepare final copies that would be stored in fine chests for generations to come. It was perhaps at this point that Kaneyoshi was singled out above all the participants by being asked to write the preface to that same official record, the kind of duty that traditionally went to the man acknowledged as the outstanding scholar of the court.

Unfortunately, the full text of this collection of ten-thousand verses has not survived, but a record of the first three verses of each of the twenty separate five-hundred-verse sequences passed down by the Konoe house preserves Kaneyoshi's preface intact, and it shows that Kaneyoshi was up to the task required of him. No one was more suited by training and predilection to compose in the expected style of such works, which served less to describe an event than to memorialize it for future generations; nor was anyone more committed to the revival of linked verse among the aristocracy. The result was a document that not only retained its importance in the history of linked verse as a poetic genre but also set a pattern that Kaneyoshi was to follow in all the years to come. The document itself is conventional in approach, tracing the history of the genre through the generations and always focusing squarely on its courtly nature, as a short excerpt describing the prelude to the grand session makes clear:

> In the spring of the year, on the ninth day of the second lunar month, Lord Yoshinori began seven days of

> ritual confinement at the Kitano Shrine, having beforehand commanded the Commander of the Gate Guards of the Right to prepare for a dedicatory sequence of ten-thousand linked verses to be composed in a single day on the eleventh of the month. . . . Thus all were gathered, from those exalted to the ranks of the stars surrounding the shrine of the Shining Sun God, to others of repute who came to take their part in the festivities.
>
> On the evening of the day previous, the participants began to arrive, some making their way over spots of bare ground where the snow had melted, others wandering through the storms far back in the mountains. As the night wore on and everyone settled down, I stole out to get a glimpse of the shrine precincts, whose venerability and air of solitude struck deep at my heart. The way the standing lanterns scattered their light was as if a sky full of stars had descended to earth. Echoing bells accompanied the sounds of voices chanting sutras, and moonlight shone on the sand like cold frost. On the east wind came the scent of plum blossoms, reminding one of nothing so much as musk cast upon the breeze.[4]

Because the purpose of such works was to record what was distinctive about any particular event than what connected it to a larger tradition, Kaneyoshi's descriptions give less attention to details of the day's events than a literary historian might wish. Yet his words succeed admirably in describing the pomp and circumstance of what, for its time, was one of the grandest of court events, and one that would be associated with the name Lord Ichijō ever after.

As attested by diaries and other records, Kaneyoshi's interest in *renga* continued after 1433, but his next ten years or so were dedicated more fully to an older genre of court poetry, the *uta.* By this time Kaneyoshi had spent years studying the history of the thirty-one-syllable form, which had provided the foundation for the development of linked verse, and he was already proving himself a worthy poet in his frequent appearances at *uta* meetings and contests. But such activities were only preparations for the prospect that presented itself in the mid-1430s, namely, to take part in the creation of an imperial anthology of the genre, a *chokusenshū*, which would be the twenty-first in a line of such works extending back to 905, the date of

4. Ibid., 315–20.

Kokinshū ("Collection of Ancient and Modern Times"). The new collection soon occupied the attentions of every worthy poet. The moving force behind the project was, as would be expected, the shogun Yoshinori, who, although obeying the precedent of having the emperor actually issue the order for work to begin, appointed the chief compiler, Asukai Masayo (1390–1452), and supported the project until its completion.[5] As ancient custom demanded, hundred-poem sequences from the major poets of the day were commissioned, and the usual rituals and ceremonies were enacted. Before long the compilation process was well under way.

Although he was among those asked to submit his work to the compilers for review, Kaneyoshi seemed in the beginning to have had little to do with the actual process of compilation, which almost immediately became entangled in fights between Masayo and members of the Reizei family, who felt that as direct descendants of Fujiwara Teika (1162–1241) they should have been given appointment as compilers above their conservative rivals in the Asukai family.[6] Toward the end of 1435, however, Kaneyoshi was asked to write the Japanese preface for the anthology; thereafter he was involved in the project in a more active way. The honor of writing such a preface had come to only a handful of men in all of Japanese history, men such as the Heian poet and scholar Ki Tsurayuki (868–945), the great poet and critic Fujiwara Shunzei (1114–1204), Kaneyoshi's own illustrious ancestor Kujō Yoshitsune (1169–1206), and, more recently, Nijō Yoshimoto. To have one's name added to such a list was to be recognized by all later ages as the outstanding scholar of an entire generation.

Before the completion of the anthology, however, Kaneyoshi was asked to write yet another preface, this one for the record of a poetry gathering at the home of the shogun held upon the occasion of a formal visit by the emperor to the shogunal palace in the tenth month of 1437.[7] Barely ten lines long, this second of his extant prefaces

5. For details of the compilation process, see Inoue Muneo, *Chūsei kadanshi no kenkyū, Muromachi zenki,* rev. ed.(Tokyo: Kasama Shoin, 1984), 110–14.
6. The Reizei could claim direct descent from Teika's son Tameie (1198–1275), whereas the Asukai could claim only that their ancestors had been literary disciples.
7. Text available in Takei Kazuto, ed. and comp., *Ichijō Kaneyoshi zenkashū* (Tokyo: Kasama Shoin, 1983), 18.

is short compared to his later efforts, but it tells us a great deal about the events of that day and also shows that Kaneyoshi was a master of the formal Chinese that was an important tool for anyone aspiring to scholarly reputation at court.

> One winter day, when I attended His Majesty on the occasion of an Imperial Progress to Muromachi Palace, I wrote a poem describing the color of pines reflected in the pond, along with this preface:
>
> Outside the East Capital—precincts sublime;
> Inside the Left Minister's estate—a garden of renown.
> There flows a stream, diverted from Duck River;
> There stands a mountain, shaped like a tortoise shell.
> Alas, could even Tai Yi Pond compare with this?
> No, not even Ji Cui could be its match!
> Here Our Lord took respite from his myriad labors,
> Carried by six dragons, proceeding at his ease;
> Just as when Han Wen Di stopped to rest his horses,
> And restored spring to the Camp of Thin Willows—
> Just as when Song Tai Zu, pondering decisions,
> Visited Han Wang's Hall in the snow.
> All virtue Our Lord inherits from former lords,
> Displaying the power of ancient rites.
> Here rose "Heavenly Strains"—before the stone steps,
> Filling our ears with the sounds of prosperous times;
> Here we heard "Heavy Dew"—on the waters of the pond,
> Delighting swallows reveling in song.
> Behold, how tall pines throw shadows on the waves,
> While Red Top and Green Locks bring long life to all!
> And how beautiful seaweed casts reflections on the waters,
> As we learn the old ways of lone goose and spotted dove![8]

The genre to which the poem belongs is the Chinese *fu*, or "rhyme prose," whose main purpose was to describe an event in lavish metaphorical terms. Thus the preface begins with praise for the palace of the shogun (Minister of the Left at the time), the precincts of which are compared with famed Chinese gardens of old. It then goes on to describe the Imperial Progress, which is likewise compared to ancient Chinese prototypes—one involving Emperor Han Wen Di

8. Ibid.

(202–157 B.C.) and the other Song Tai Zu (A.D. 927–76), first emperor of the Song Dynasty. The preface concludes with ornate allusions to the artistic activities of the day, which other records indicate to have featured an elegant program in which the participants were divided into three groups in boats on the pond in the shogun's garden—one composing Japanese poems, another Chinese poems, and a third providing music.[9] Throughout, the tone is lofty, the language erudite, leaving one with the suspicion that Kaneyoshi's record of the gathering may improve upon the actual events that it describes.

We do not know how Kaneyoshi's short preface was received by his contemporaries at court and in the shogunal offices, but that it was not judged a failure is evident from the fact that just a few months later he was requested to write an additional preface—this one in Chinese—for the upcoming imperial anthology that was now nearly complete. Whatever the motivation for the second request, it meant that the Ichijō heir would become only the second person in Japanese history to contribute two prefaces to an imperial anthology, the first having been Emperor Hanazono (1297–1348) nearly a century before.[10]

The historical record indicates that Kaneyoshi quite outdid himself in penning the Chinese preface that Ashikaga Yoshinori requested, producing a work so laden with obscure characters that

9. Some further notes, by line: 3: "Duck River" is the Kamo River, which ran along the eastern border of the capital. 4: "Shape of a tortoise shell" is a phrase involving the Chinese character for *shina,* three square "mouths" that resemble the pattern on the animal's back and that can also be read "third rank," referring here to the courtly rank of the shogun. 5 and 6: Both Tai Yi and Ji Cui are names of famous ponds in the palaces of Chinese emperors. 8: The horses that pulled the imperial cart were referred to as dragons. 9 and 10: "Camp of Thin Willows" refers to a garrison whose noble general was visited by Han Wen Di, who brought peace to the kingdom after a period of warfare. 11 and 12: Song Tai Zu once braved a snowstorm to consult with General Han Wang before making an important decision. 15–18: *Jun tian* ("Heavenly Strains") is the music of the gods, and *Zhan lu* ("Heavy Dew") is a song recorded in the *Shi jing.* 20: Red Top is an epithet for the red-crowned crane, and Green Locks for the tortoise, both symbols of longevity. 22: Both the "lone goose" and the "spotted dove" are metaphors for the properly reticent gentleman.

10. The emperor wrote the prefaces for *Fūgashū* ("Collection of Elegance," 1344–46), the seventeenth imperial anthology.

the shogun asked for it to be revised before its final submission.[11] The Japanese preface, on the other hand, was accepted without emendation. Its gentle cadences, as evident in this short excerpt, were evidently music to his cohort's ears.

> Since that ancient time when a poem of thirty-one syllables was first composed amongst the eightfold clouds of Izumo, the poetry of Yamato has been a medium for lauding the imperial reign, pacifying the people, paying court, and voicing the thoughts of one's heart. For generation upon generation, all who have come to this place—whether high or low, wise or ignorant—have learned the art of poetry, and never has there been a time when it was not avidly pursued throughout the land. Hence it is that, on twenty-one occasions, from the time of *Man'yōshū* and the imperial court at Nara—whose name calls to mind the mighty oak—until the splendid age of the Eitoku era, poems have been chosen and gathered by official order as records of their times.
>
> Moreover, the number of poems stored away elsewhere, like seaweed from our country's many bays, would surely fill more than a thousand boxes, and five great carts could not bear away the leaves of words stored in the noble houses. Yet the more one draws from the wellsprings of the heart, the more those springs gush forth; the more one harvests in the forests of words, the thicker those groves become. Truly it is in the art of poetry that we find reds richer than the red of autumn leaves and blues deeper than the blue of the indigo plant.[12]

So much of both the style and content of Kaneyoshi's phrases derives from earlier prefaces that his work cannot be considered original; but it was erudition, not imagination, that the project demanded, and this the former regent provided. Moreover, when the collection was completed, he was also pleased to find he and his family well represented among the poems of what was to be the last

11. For details, see entries for Eikyō 11.6.27–29 in *Kennaiki,* the diary of Madenokōji Tokifusa (1394–1457) (*Kennaiki,* 2d ed., in *Dai nihon kokiroku,* 10 vols. [Tokyo: Iwanami Shoten, 1987]).
12. *Shin shokukokinshū,* in Taniyama Shigeru et al., eds., *Shinpen kokka taikan,* vol. 1 (Tokyo: Kadokawa Shoten, 1983), 722.

of the imperial collections. Kaneyoshi and his father were honored with nine poems each—less than Yoshinori and the leaders of the Asukai house, but more than Gyōkō (1391–1455), another bastion of the conservative school, or even Ashikaga Yoshimitsu. Even Kaneyoshi's maternal grandfather, Higashinobōjō Hidenaga, was remembered with two poems. More importantly, though, as the contributor of the prefaces Kaneyoshi was again connected to the work for all future times as sponsor and patron, in a ritual if not a literal sense: the anthology would bear the honor of his name, even if the paper on which it was written and the lacquer box in which it was stored were bought with the shogun's money.

Despite these honors, the late 1430s and early 1440s were trying times for Kaneyoshi and many others at court because of the increasingly rash behavior of the shogun Yoshinori. Even the imperial anthology showed signs of his bad humor in the total exclusion of some of those who had offended him, particularly Reizei Mochitame (1401–54) and Shōtetsu (1381–1459) of the liberal school. Now hardly a month went by without some hapless courtier suffering public humiliation, the confiscation of his estates, or temporary confinement by the shogun's order. Some were even murdered by Yoshinori's assassins. Thus, while the arts continued with the support of the great families and the shogunate, the atmosphere was one of fear. Kaneyoshi retired to his study, where he concentrated on finding appropriate livings for his children and on his usual occupation of scholarship.[13]

Yoshinori's excesses did not last long. In 1441 he was cut down in the same way that he had disposed of many his own enemies—by a group of assassins who surrounded him during a Noh performance at the home of Akamatsu Mitsusuke (1381–1441). The court was shocked, of course; some lamented a political situation that could allow such events to happen. But no one except his own immediate vassals

13. Yoshinori's bad temper was legendary even in his own time. For accounts of how two of Kaneyoshi's close relatives—Higashinobōjō Masunaga (1407–74), a first cousin, and Nakamikado Toshisuke—suffered at the shogun's hands, see entries for Eikyō 2.11.9 and Eikyō 8.2.12 in *Kanmon gyoki,* the diary of Fushiminoya Sadafusa (Go-Sukō'in, 1372-1456). Another courtier, Hino Yoshisuke, father of Katsumitsu, was even less fortunate: *Kanmon gyoki,* Eikyō 6.6.9–6.6.12, records that he was murdered in his bed upon Yoshinori's order (*Kanmon gyoki,* 2 vols. [Tokyo: Gunsho Ruijū Kanseikai]).

mourned the shogun's passing. Within months those who had withdrawn into seclusion to avoid his wrath were allowed to return to public life, and the capital regained a semblance of peace and order.

Almost as if to celebrate the removal of the *aku shogun* ("evil shogun") as an impediment to the peaceful conduct of courtly affairs, Kaneyoshi sponsored a grand literary event in the old style—an *uta-awase* of the sort that had not been known in the capital for almost three decades. Invitations to poets went out in late 1442. Finally, twenty-eight people appeared for the gathering, which was held at Kaneyoshi's home on First Avenue in the middle of the second lunar month of 1443; the contest ran for 280 rounds. Among the participants were many of Kaneyoshi's family and stewards; also in attendance were several military types. Most conspicuous about the contest, however, was its partisan support of those who had been so cruelly served by the deceased shogun, especially the members of the Reizei family and Shōtetsu. Although invited, Asukai Masanaga, a younger poet of the conservative faction, sent his poems but did not show up for the event. And the more senior Asukai poets, most conspicuously Masayo himself, also failed to attend. This left Gyōkō alone to argue for the aesthetic and stylistic principles of the Nijō line.[14]

Exactly when Kaneyoshi himself had become a Reizei partisan is a matter of debate. That his son and heir Norifusa (1423–80) took a daughter of Reizei Tameyuki (d. 1439) as his principal wife around this time, however, shows his desire for affiliation with the cause of the liberal school in the most fundamental of ways. And in the preface and judgments of the 1443 *uta-awase* he had little patience for the staid doctrines of the Asukai family. Colophons of the text of the contest show that wins and losses were decided by a vote of the participants (*shūgihan*), but it was Kaneyoshi who, after the event, wrote up the actual judgments and the preface, which show both his erudition and his impatience with the narrow-mindedness of the conservative camp. For the rest of his life he remained a champion of the Reizei house, providing support through poetry meetings and the gift of his prestige in court affairs. Records show him in gatherings with Shōtetsu and Mochitame frequently. In later years he served as

14. For a text of this contest, called *Saki no sesshō-ke uta-awase* ("The Poem Contest at the Home of the Former Regent"), see vol. 5 of *Shinpen kokka taikan*.

judge for a number of other poem contests, some for contests held in the imperial palace, and he also served as judge again on many occasions. Gyōkō and the Asukai were incensed but could do little to thwart so high a noble, especially after Kaneyoshi's appointment as regent again in 1447.[15]

In the new atmosphere of openness that came with the temporary hiatus in shogunal power, Kaneyoshi also lent his support to linked verse and linked-verse poets. It seems to have been around this time, for instance, that he struck up a literary partnership with Sōzei, a student of Shōtetsu who acted as Commissioner of *Renga* (*bugyō*) for the shogunate from 1448 until just before his death in 1455 and with whom Kaneyoshi had been acquainted since at least 1444.[16] Together the two men collaborated on a number of projects, including an important revision of the rules of composition (*Shinshiki kon'an,* "New Ideas on the Rules," 1452), the composition of several sequences according to by then antiquated rules and methods, and the compilation of a new and very large collection of linked verse intended to be submitted as a second imperial anthology of the genre entitled the *Shingyokushū* ("New Collection of Gems").[17] After Sōzei's death, Kaneyoshi continued his work with linked-verse poets, particularly Sōgi (1421–1502), one of Sōzei's foremost disciples. In his day Kaneyoshi was in fact one of the chief noble patrons of a whole generation of *rengashi,* whose art could well use the public support of a man who had through his many scholarly lectures and treatises, as well as his creative work in poetry, become one of the greatest court figures of all time.

15. For a complete account of all Kaneyoshi's activities in poetic circles, see Takei, *Ichijō Kaneyoshi zenkashū*. The most famous of the other poetry contests in which he acted as judge are the *Bunnan sannen shika-awase* of 1446, which was sponsored by Fushinomiya Sadafusa (Go-Sukō'in), and the *Hōtoku ninen sendō uta-awase,* in which he shared judging duties with Asukai Masayo. For details, see Inoue, *Chūsei kadanshi no kenkyū,* 145–47. A version of the latter annotated by Itō Kei is available in *Chūsei wakashū, Muromachi hen,* vol. 47 of *Shin nihon koten bungaku taikei* (Tokyo: Iwanami Shoten, 1990).

16. *Yasutomi no ki* for Bunnan 1.2.30 lists Sōzei as one of the auditors of Kaneyoshi's lectures on *Genji monogatari* (*Yasutomi no ki,* vols. 37-40 of *Shiryō taisei* [Tokyo: Rinsen Shoten, 1965]).

17. The later source is a preface Kaneyoshi wrote for Sōgi's *renga* anthology, *Chikurinshō*. See n. 21 below.

By the mid-1460s, however, the court was facing perilous times. As is well known, internecine strife among the military clans was once again the main cause of trouble. The Ōnin War—the name given to a series of conflicts that laid waste the northern part of the capital—erupted in 1467 and sent most of the high aristocracy into temporary exile. Kaneyoshi's house and library were ransacked, and not only the manuscript of his huge *renga* anthology but also thousands of Chinese and Japanese classics were lost.[18] At first Kaneyoshi, who had been made regent for the third time just before the beginning of hostilities, tried to stay in the capital, hoping for a quick resolution of the conflict. But late in the eighth month he fled, with his large family, to the Zuishin-in, a temple located on the southern outskirts of the city, where one of his sons was serving as abbot. Six months later, when fighting spread to that area, he went on to Nara, where he stayed for the next ten years in one of the residences of the Daijō-in, a *monzeki* ("cloister") over which another son, known as Jinson (1430–1508), presided as chief priest. Since the abbots of the various subtemples of the great Nara conclaves were nearly all sons of noble families, the residences were designed to accommodate the noble lifestyle, allowing for privacy and the pursuit of artistic interests. Kaneyoshi's own residence, the Jōju-in, consisted of a large main building, wings connected by walkways, a meeting hall, various appendages for kitchen space and storage, and an ornamental garden. In all, it was a home away from home where he would stay for most of the next decade.

In Nara, Kaneyoshi lived a fairly quiet life, devoting himself again to scholarship. It was at this time that he produced his famous commentaries on *Genji monogatari* and *Nihon shoki,* as well as a famous hundred-poem sequence (*Nanto hyakushu,* "One Hundred Poems from the Southern Capital," 1473), an important essay on linked verse (*Fude no susabi,* "Amusements with My Brush," 1469), and an encyclopedic *renga* handbook (*Renjugappekishū*, "Strings of Linked Jewels," 1469). Although the needs of his large entourage—which included at least three wives, a number of children, and servants—strained the resources of the Daijō-in, he seems to have lived in relative comfort. Family matters, notably the placement of more

18. Motoori Norinaga puts the number of Kaneyoshi's manuscripts at 30,000. For details, see Nagashima, *Ichijō Kanera,* 40–45, 96.

children in temples and the handling of finances, were a preoccupation, of course. But his artistic and scholarly interests still seem to have taken much of his time. Visitors, including other nobles likewise seeking refuge in the peaceful ancient capital and also poets and artists, came regularly.

Unfortunately, Kaneyoshi's diary (assuming, that is, that he kept one) did not survive the devastation of his age; however, for the period of his stay in Nara we do have the record of Jinson, who recorded enough information about his father's activities to give us a clear idea of how the old man spent his time at the Jōju-in. A few entries from 1471 and 1472 suffice to show that he was still very much involved in cultural and political affairs.

1471

1.26: Kaneyoshi sends samurai to the capital to query about the posthumous name to be given to Retired Emperor Hikohito, recently deceased.

2.4: Kaneyoshi's daughter Tsuneko becomes the wife of Takatsukasa Fusahira.

2.5: Kaneyoshi holds a *renga* session at Jōju-in.

2.6: Kaneyoshi suggests the names Go-Hanazono or Go-Tsuchimikado for Retired Emperor.

2.30: Kaneyoshi receives a gift of two thousand bolts of silk and robes from Saitō Myōchin.

3.15–17: Kaneyoshi leads entourage, including sons and retainers, on excursion to see cherry blossoms at various famous sites in Nara, holding *renga* and *uta* parties along the way.

3.20–23: Kaneyoshi goes on a blossom-viewing excursion to Yoshino with his wife and others.

5.9: Kaneyoshi and Jinson observe thirteenth-year memorial services for the poet Shōtetsu.

Intercalary 8.15: Nakamikado Nobutane comes from Kyoto to Nara for safety and visits Daijō-in.

Intercalary 8.21: Kaneyoshi's daughter Tsuneko gives birth to a girl.

9.19–10.8: Kaneyoshi gives lectures on *Kokinshū* at Jōju-in, at the request of Nakamikado Nobutane.

11.8: Kaneyoshi's wife Sanjō Tsubone puts on a formal sash in her fifth month of pregnancy at formal ceremony held at Jōju-in.

1472

1.1: Kaneyoshi hosts a new year gathering with his wives, Jinson, several other sons and daughters, retainers, and others.

1.14: Kaneyoshi holds a tea ceremony at Jōju-in.
2.6–14: Kaneyoshi attends a torchlight Noh performance by the Konparu, Hosshō, and Kanze schools at Kōfukuji.
3.2: A girl-child is born to Sanjō Tsubone at Jōju-in, the twenty-fifth of Kaneyoshi's children.
3.3: Kaneyoshi participates in a *renga* session at Jōdoji.
3.5: Kaneyoshi participates in a monthly *renga* session at Daijō-in.
5.27: Kaneyoshi writes an inscription for a portrait of Ōuchi Masahiro.
8.7: Kaneyoshi pays a formal visit to Kasuga Shrine to pray for the health of his new child.
8.24: Kaneyoshi's fifteen-year-old daughter takes the tonsure at Jōju-in, then goes into service at Hokkeji as nun.
10.25: Kaneyoshi bids farewell to his first wife, Shōrinjidono, who leaves to take up residence in Mino.
12.20: Kaneyoshi conducts a coming-of-age ceremony for his son and heir Fuyuyoshi at Jōju-in.[19]

Although these entries disclose a few facts about Kaneyoshi's domestic difficulties, financial and otherwise, they also make it apparent that his interest in poetry and the arts continued unabated. No doubt any costs incurred from his "sponsorship" of Noh performances, *renga* sessions, and so forth, were borne by the Daijō-in and not himself, but the fact remains that even as a refugee he still wielded influence sufficient to support an active cultural life. Regardless of the state of his ancestral house back in Kyoto, the government still consulted him on important courtly affairs, and requests still came for the use of his name—to adorn a portrait of the daimyo Ōuchi Masahiro (1446–95), or, as we know from another source, to provide an appropriate inscription for a painting by the prominent artist Shūbun (fl. 1430–50).[20]

It is not surprising, therefore, to learn that it was also during this period that Kaneyoshi wrote three of his most famous prefaces. The first was for a linked-verse contest (*Kitabatake-ke renga-awase,* "The Linked-Verse Contest of the Kitabatake House," 1469) involving Major Counselor Kitabatake Noritomo (1423–71), some of the latter's

19. See *Daijō-in jisha zōjiki,* 12 vols., in *Zoku shiryō taisei* (Tokyo: Rinsen Shoten, 1978).
20. Takei, *Ichijō Kaneyoshi zenkashū,* 194. Nagashima, *Ichijō Kanera,* 68–69 displays a photocopy of the actual legend and a printed copy of its text.

vassals, and a group of *rengashi,* including Sōgi, who brought the work to Kaneyoshi from the Kitabatake estates in Ise with a request for a preface and his judgments of the poems themselves. Kaneyoshi finished the job in the first month of 1470, leaving literary historians one of their few records of *uta-awase*-style competition in linked verse.[21]

In 1473 another poet came to Nara with a similar request: Shōkō (1412–93), the chief disciple of Shōtetsu, asked Kaneyoshi to write a preface for *Sōkonshū,* the personal collection of his deceased master. Kaneyoshi had known Shōtetsu since the first part of the century, it would seem, and the poet had been one of the Reizei-school poets he had supported in the 1440s and early 1450s. Kaneyoshi granted Shōkō's request, producing a short introduction for what, at 11,236 poems, became the largest of all medieval *shikashū,* or personal anthologies.[22]

The last of Kaneyoshi's most important prefaces was written in 1476 for an anthology of poems by the greatest *renga* masters of the mid-fifteenth century, including his old friend Sōzei. Entitled *Chikurinshō* ("Bamboo Grove Collection"), it was compiled by Sōgi, who was by this time becoming one of Kaneyoshi's most trusted and valued students. As the preface notes, Kaneyoshi's own plans for a new imperial anthology of linked verse had been postponed due to the destruction of his library years before, and Sōgi's work gave him an opportunity to support in a concrete way one of the literary arts to which he had dedicated himself for the past forty years.[23]

> A foolish old man, attracted by the fine scents of earlier times, went about gathering fragments of words left behind, choosing ten thousand verses and making them into a twenty-volume book named *New Collection of Gems.* But as he was waiting for an imperial decree following the example of the *Tsukuba Collection,* with his fascicles stored in the library of the Peach Blossom Manse, the great disturbance of the

21. Unfortunately, only rounds 140–250 of this contest have been preserved. See Fukui Kyūzō, *Renga bungaku no kenkyū* (Tokyo: Kikuya Shoten, 1948), 273–322.
22. For a copy of Shōtetsu's anthology with Kaneyoshi's preface, see vol. 5 of *Shikashū taisei* (Tokyo: Meiji Shoin, 1983), 532–887
23. Hoshika Muneichi, ed., *Kōhon chikurinshō* (Tokyo: Iwanami Shoten, 1937).

> Ōnin era erupted, and he heard that not only had his weed-choked house become a burnt-over field, but also that white waves had arisen and scattered his seven hundred boxes of manuscripts like fish thrown from their homes, leaving them as so much refuse on the roadside. Thus the light of his new gems disappeared, left as heavy dew on the cogon grass.
>
> Then appeared a certain recluse monk called Sōgi, who had gathered the linked verses of seven men, making a collection of ten volumes, which he titled *Bamboo Grove Collection.* His selections seemed to show proper sensitivity, and I immediately consented to his request that I write a few words for him. If the dewlike life of this old man now adrift on the waves of old age should last long enough, I have it in mind to compile a sequel to the *Tsukuba Collection,* in which case this *Bamboo Grove Collection* may serve as a source from which to choose verses, in the way of the private anthologies of the past.

It is worth noting that here Kaneyoshi does not simply cede his duties to his student but expresses his intent to remain an active patron, as Sōgi must have remembered nearly twenty years later when he asked Kaneyoshi's son and heir Fuyuyoshi (1464–1514) to provide the preface for *Shinsen tsukubashū* ("New Tsukuba Collection," 1495), the second imperially recognized anthology of linked verse.

Thus, near the end of his life Kaneyoshi could look back on an involvement in artistic patronage, although of a special and rather limited kind, rivaled by no one else of his generation. For although his resources even in the early years did not allow him to sponsor the sorts of enterprises that many of his ancestors had thought of as commonplace, Kaneyoshi could still claim to have endorsed with his name the only imperial *uta* anthology of his time, four of the major documents of the linked-verse tradition, several of the most important *uta-awase* of the late medieval age, and the personal anthology of one of the most important poets of the Muromachi period. One might argue, of course, that such support was patronage in name only. But it would be hard to overemphasize the importance of a noble name and status in the late medieval period—a fact that those who came to Kaneyoshi asking for prefaces probably never doubted. It was not only out of friendship that men such as Shōkō and Sōgi came to Nara. Both understood that attaching Kaneyoshi's name to a literary document gave that work a kind of prestige and authority it could gain in no other way.[24] And even though this was probably less true in the case of those who came to ask for prefaces to the *Kitano manku* and the *Shin shokukokinshū*—works for which it was a particular honor to write the preface—it is certain that even on those occasions Kaneyoshi was looked upon as the most appropriate man for such a task partly because of the prominence of his name and the influence of his station.

Even as an exile in Nara, then, Kaneyoshi continued the practice of lending his name to literary projects. This was a pattern he had set early in life; the financial crisis of his last years did little to change it. For the sake of accuracy, however, it must be admitted that the Ōnin War marked a change in Kaneyoshi's fortunes, as it did for almost everyone associated with the noble families. Even before the outbreak of hostilities, he had experienced trouble in securing revenues from his estates; now the flow of money and goods came to an abrupt halt. If not for the resources of the Daijō-in, he would have been reduced to utter destitution. Even with Jinson's support, he was forced to spend a good deal of his time in seeking funds to support his aristocratic lifestyle.

With this change in his financial situation came a change in the design of his patronage. Indeed, it was at this time that the Kaneyoshi of popular historical narrative was born: the beleaguered former regent (he resigned that post for the last time in the early fall of 1470) forced to rely on gifts from traveling poets and warlords for his sustenance. Even the picture he presents of himself in Nara written at the time does much to support the conception of him as *regent redux*:

> Since the Enryaku era, when the court was moved from the capital at Nara to the broad Kyoto moors, over fifty sovereigns have ruled the land, and during that time the winds over the reed plains have often grown stormy, blowing the blossoms into disarray. . . . Yet our present disturbance of the Ōnin era has neither precedent in the past nor likely rival in the future. Within the ninefold streets of the city, everything to the north of Second Avenue—the Ministry of State, the Department of Shrines, all of the hundred

24. For a discussion of the importance of Kaneyoshi's name to the reputation of a book, see Inada Toshiyori, *Shōtetsu no kenkyū, chūsei kajin no kenkyū* (Tokyo: Kasama Shoin, 1976), 275–76.

> offices, indeed, everything but the palaces of the emperor and his royal father—has gone like the smoke over the Palace of Xianyang, leaving a field rich only with the dew of Gusu. What wise man can have done such a thing as to lay waste to the ranks of the great houses, reducing their frames to nothing? The halls and towers of the Eastern and Western hills, with their lines of tile roofs that looked like the columns in a beehive, are now burned to the ground or broken in pieces, leaving not a blade of grass amidst ruins buried in the eightfold clouds.
>
> In the midst of all this was a hapless old man who had lived long in a place named for its peach blossoms. As his house was located on the border between the two camps, people warned him that he would not be able to stay on there, and so he locked up his weed-bound gate and left like all the rest, taking refuge for a time in a place near Ninth Avenue. When he looked back to the place he had left behind, he saw smoke rising above it, reducing it to a burnt-over field. Thanks to its tiled roof and earthen walls, his library escaped the spreading flames, but soon thieves gathered around and, perhaps thinking that the place must contain great treasures, broke in and rifled through every one of the hundreds of boxes of manuscripts, which they tossed aside like high breakers scattering fish. In the end, not a single volume of the Chinese and Japanese documents preserved by the family for more than ten generations escaped. The old man was left like an aging crane without a nest, like a blind man bereft of his cane.
>
> Having heard that things were not likely to calm down anywhere in the capital soon, I left my lodgings on Ninth Avenue toward the end of the Month of Leaves in the second year of the Ōnin era, yearning for the ancient capital at Nara. Full of gratitude for the blessings of the Kasuga God, I borrowed lodgings in priests' quarters at the foot of Mikasa Mountain, where battle cries faded into the distance, allowing an old man some hope for a little peaceful sleep. There, with the last leaves of my family tree scattered hither and yon, I have spent my days like a withered tree covered with frost.[25]

If the image of Kaneyoshi as a beggar reduced to depending upon others for his sustenance is a distortion, then it is a distortion

25. The passage is taken from *Fude no susabi* ("Amusements with My Brush," 1470). See Kidō Saizō, ed., *Rengaronshū 3* (Tokyo: Miyai Shoten, 1985), 151–54.

that he is partially responsible for creating, both here and in the preface to Sōgi's anthology. And that there is some truth to the popular understanding of Kaneyoshi's last years is impossible to refute. As has been well documented, it was at this time that Kaneyoshi used the services of Sōgi as a messenger and agent. More than once the traveling *renga* master brought his teacher gifts of cash, and it was Sōgi too who often carried the former regent's requests for funds and other kinds of assistance to other possible benefactors.[26] Thus, the idea of a former regent and chieftain of the Fujiwara clan reduced to dependence on people with whom in earlier ages a regent would seldom have allowed a face-to-face audience has some basis in fact. Even before this time patronage had implied some sort of reciprocation, but now the forms of that reciprocation were more tangible—usually meaning money or services.

It is important to remember, however, that not all of Kaneyoshi's benefactors were of such low status. Indeed, it can be argued that it was an aristocratic family, the Hino, that was of most help to Kaneyoshi in his times of trouble. His relationship with them had been forged long before he left the capital for Nara, and until his death he looked to that family more than any other for support. For that reason alone, the members of that clan, a minor branch of the Fujiwara, deserve some attention as patrons of scholars and artists in general and of Kaneyoshi in particular.

In earlier ages, the Hino family—one of the so-called *seigake,* whose heirs could rise no higher than Major Counselor in government administration—had been one of the lesser court clans, distinguished only by its status as a provider of wives for the Ashikaga shoguns. During the time of Ashikaga Yoshinori, who took a Hino wife only under protest, the family had in fact been under censure. But after Yoshinori's murder the Hino had been among the first to take advantage of the political confusion leading up to the Ōnin War. Thus it was that in 1455, the new shogun, Yoshimasa (1435–90), took Hino Tomiko (1440–96) as his principal wife. Younger sister to Hino Katsumitsu (1429–76), Tomiko turned out to be as strong-willed and adept a politician as her brother. The two of them, either one of whom would have been too much for the retiring Yoshimasa to handle, dominated the political affairs of the court for the next half century. Indeed,

26. See Nagashima, *Ichijō Kanera,* 20, 65–74, 80–82, 113–15.

much of the blame for the Ōnin War was due to their endless machinations. Shattering precedents in the process, Katsumitsu had himself appointed Palace Minister in 1467; nine years later, in 1476, he was made Minister of the Left, a scandalous advancement that earned him the title *oshidaijin* ("minister by force") among his betters in the higher-ranking families.[27]

Katsumitsu died less than a month after his audacious appointment, but Tomiko lived on for twenty years, becoming one of the dominant powers in the capital. In her first years as Yoshimasa's wife, she had managed to eliminate most of her rivals through intrigue and deception. After her husband's retirement into the Eastern Hills, she continued to rule through her son Yoshihisa (1465–89), the reigning shogun. Her financial ventures, which included moneylending, attempts at control of the rice market, and control of the toll gates at the entrances to the city, made her rich. And with her money she kept an elegant court, supporting poets, artists, and scholars—one of the few things upon which she and Yoshimasa could agree.

Exactly when Kaneyoshi first became acquainted with Katsumitsu and Tomiko is not entirely clear. Records indicate that he owed his appointment as regent for the second time to the intervention of Hino Shigeko (d. 1463), widow of Yoshinori and aunt of Tomiko and Katsumitsu.[28] While regent, he of course had close contact with Katsumitsu, whose home stood on the northeast corner of Kaneyoshi's lot in northern Kyoto. It was Kaneyoshi who directed the *haiga* (a formal celebration marking a new officer's assumption of title and duties) for Katsumitsu's appointment in early 1467 as Palace Minister, just several months before Kaneyoshi's last appointment as regent.[29] Finally, it was flames spreading from the Hino mansion that destroyed Kaneyoshi's house during the first days of the Ōnin War.[30] Even after Kaneyoshi's move to Nara, he kept in touch with Katsumitsu.

It was with Kaneyoshi's final return to Kyoto in 1477, some months after Katsumitsu's passing, that the relationship between the former regent, newly tonsured under the monkish name Kakukei, and

27. For details of Hino family history through the time of Tomiko, see Kawai Masaharu, *Ashikaga Yoshimasa* (Tokyo: Kiyomizu Shoten, 1972) and Yoshimura Teiji, *Hino Tomiko* (Tokyo: Chūō Kōron, 1985)

28. Nagashima, *Ichijō Kanera,* 38–39.

29. See *Daijō-in jisha zōjiki,* Bunshō 2.2.25–Bunshō 2.3.11.

30. Ibid., Ōnin 1.9.18..

the Hino took on noteworthy proportions. Only after repeated requests from the emperor and assurances of lodging and revenue from Yoshimasa did Kaneyoshi come back to the capital, where, of course, his former home was still nothing but a pile of ashes. At first he stayed in a temple, then in the quarters of a vassal of Hosokawa Masamoto (1466–1507), and finally in a small house just east of the ruins of the shogun's Palace of Flowers. Despite his good intentions, Yoshimasa was not able to revive the flow of estate revenues, and even plans to reconstruct the Ichijō mansion on its old property went awry when lumber sent for the project from Tosa was appropriated in transit by Hatakeyama Yoshinari (d. 1490?), another of the major combatants of the Ōnin War.[31]

It was in this context, then, that Kaneyoshi turned most conspicuously from literary patron to beneficiary—not so much of lower class poets, however, as of the shogunal house. Before, he had favored poets among the military and priestly classes with his lectures on the classics and on the esoteric traditions of the court; now he became a sort of private tutor to Hino Tomiko and her son the shogun, no doubt with the expectation of tangible kinds of support in return. *Daijō-in jisha zōjiki* records him lecturing on *Genji monogatari* to Tomiko in 1478, as well as to some literati of the military clans.[32] Whether he received any direct remuneration for such activities is unknown, but Nagashima Fukutarō concludes that the house across from the grounds of the Palace of Flowers came to him as a result of Tomiko's good will.[33] Even if the nature of the payment is not certain, it seems clear that part of his motive in undertaking such enterprises was to ensure the sympathy of Tomiko toward the uncertain future of the Ichijō clan.

Nor did Kaneyoshi's duties stop at lectures: three of his final scholarly essays—*Sayo no nezame* ("Awake in the Night," 1479), *Bunmei ittōki* ("Unification in the Bunmei Era," 1479), and *Shōdan chiyō* ("Necessities for Good Government," 1480)—were written at the request of either Tomiko or her son, Yoshihisa.[34] All three belong to the genre of *teikin ōrai* ("garden precepts"), presenting cautionary

31. Nagashima, *Ichijō Kanera,* 74.
32. Ibid., 18–20, 125–26.
33. Ibid., 127–28.
34. All three works are available in Hanawa Hokiichi and Kawamata Keiichi, comps., *Shinkō gunsho ruijū,* vol. 21, 2d ed. (Tokyo: Meichō Fukyūkai, 1977–78).

remarks on a number of topics ranging from the proper conduct of government and the control of *shugo daimyō* to the evils of drink and the censure of *ashigaru,* those brigands who had wreaked such havoc during the Ōnin War. The one thing all three works have in common is that each seeks out precedents to justify *onna seiji,* "government by women." Drawing on the examples of the sun goddess Amaterasu and Hōjō Masako (1157–1225), Kaneyoshi argues that from the beginning of Japanese history women have had an appropriate role in government:

> In general, women follow their parents when they are young, their husbands as adults, and their sons in old age; thus, they do not make a name for themselves in the world. They are to be gentle and pliant. But this land of Japan is called *wakoku* ("a land of harmony and peace"), a place that should be governed by women.[35]

The strain between Confucian ideals and the reality of Tomiko's role in government is obvious. And there were some among the noble classes that criticized Kaneyoshi for catering to the tastes of his benefactors, meaning both Tomiko and the military families.[36] Modern scholars, however, tend to accept Kaneyoshi's statements as sincere, noting the influence of *Gukanshō* ("Notes on My Foolish Views") on his understanding of government and stressing that Kaneyoshi was nothing if not a realist.[37]

In the end, Kaneyoshi's tutoring of Tomiko and Yoshihisa did him less good than one might expect. His house on First Avenue was not rebuilt until after his death, and his trip in 1479 to Echizen in a vain attempt to recover some of his estate revenues from Asakura Takakage (1428–81) (in order to give his heir Fuyuyoshi [or Fuyura] a proper *haiga* celebration upon his elevation to Captain of the Right) shows how thoroughly desperate the family had become. Upon his death, the family was hard pressed to provide him with even the simplest of noble funerals.[38]

In addition to the works mentioned here, Kaneyoshi wrote a number of books and essays on court lore and custom and commen-

35. Quoted in Nagashima, *Ichijō Kanera,* 129.
36. *Daijō-in jisha zōjiki,* Bunmei 10.4.25.
37. Nagashima, *Ichijō Kanera,* 125–26, and Kawai, *Ashikaga Yoshimasa,* 132.
38. Nagashima, *Ichijō Kanera,* 84–88.

taries on the classics. Many of these are still read by specialists and scholars interested in a medieval perspective. Ironically, then, it is in his role as a representative figure of the declining years of the court, as a melancholy figure representing a profound sense of lost dreams, an expression of the medieval idea of *mujō* ("ephemerality"), that his name has survived. It should be remembered, however, that the same man who portrays himself as a hapless old man in one essay says this in another:

> It is the fate of all men to struggle to outlast the dew on the morning glory, their lives as fleeting as the dayfly's. Yet still there have been many men, both now and in the past, who by nurturing their spirits and taking care of their bodies have extended their lives to a hundred years. Surely no treasure is more precious than life itself. What living thing does not make every effort to go on living?[39]

This Kaneyoshi, this regent of stubborn will who here seeks to distinguish himself from ever-lamenting recluses such as Kamo Chōmei (1153–1216) or Yoshida Kenkō (1283–1352?), is doubtless the one who was best known in his own day and among the members of his own class. For Ichijō Kaneyoshi, known by his contemporaries at various times in his career not only by literary or pen names but also as Lord Ichijō, the Ichijō Regent, the Taikō (Great Lord), and Zenkō (Great Lord and Lay Monk), was, after all, the scion of a great clan whose past accomplishments it was his business to emulate, an expectation that he did his best to fulfill during his over sixty years of service at court.[40] And it is not insignificant that a short summation of his accomplishments written after his death should list, after his high offices and privileges, comments about his dedication to the courtly arts via his work as a writer of prefaces:

> 1437.10.21: On the occasion of an imperial progress to the Muromachi Palace, he wrote both Chinese and Japanese

39. From *Sayo no nezame* ("Awake in the Night," 1473?), in *Shinkō gunsho ruijū*, vol. 17, 171.
40. The title Taikō was used of a former regent who retained inspection powers or whose son was acting as regent; Zenkō referred to a former regent who had taken the tonsure as a lay monk without withdrawing from the world completely.

> poems for *The Poetry Meeting in Three Boats,* thereafter presenting a Japanese preface for the record to the throne.
>
> 1439: Composed on imperial command both the Japanese and Chinese prefaces for the imperial collection *Shin shokukokinshū.*
>
> 1433: Composed upon shogunal command the preface to the *Kitano ichinichi ichimanku renga.*[41]

To conclude, one need only say that Kaneyoshi is also remembered as a patron of poets, from Shōtetsu and Mochitame to Sōzei and Sōgi, whose name the latter rightly valued as the symbol of one of the most powerful literary patrons of Japan's late medieval age.

41. Nagashima, *Ichijō Kanera,* 90–92.

The Poet Shōkō and the Salons Of Sakai

Tsurusaki Hirō
Translated by Steven D. Carter

Numerous studies have established the important place of traveling *rengashi,* or "masters of linked verse," in the culture of late medieval Japan. Yet clearly there were other important "professionals" in that same age, including Noh dramatists, tea masters, and even poets in the older poetic genre known as *uta.* This chapter will provide a sketch of the activities of one distinguished member of this last group, the *uta* poet Shōkō (1412-93), concentrating particularly on his relationships with men of the port city of Sakai.

Shōkō was born in 1412, but the place of his birth is unknown. At the age of thirteen he became a disciple of Shōtetsu (1381–1459), the man whom most scholars consider to be the greatest *uta* poet of the fifteenth century. Shōkō served the older man as a disciple for the next three and a half decades, until Shōtetsu's death in 1459. During that time Shōkō composed a great deal of poetry himself, much of which is recorded in his personal anthology, *Shōkashū* ("Collection from Beneath the Pines"),[1] the earliest poems of which are dated 1424.

As Shōtetsu's artistic heir, Shōkō gained a name for himself in the *kadan,* or "poetic salons," of his day, receiving invitations to the monthly poetry meetings of the shogun's deputy, Hosokawa Katsumoto (1430–73), and traveling as far as Hakata at the request of Ōuchi Norihiro (1420–65) in 1464. But because of the Ōnin War (1467–77), Shōkō left the capital and went to Nara, where he visited Ichijō

1. The text of *Shōkashū* is available in Wakashi Kenkyūkai, comp., *Shikashū taisei,* vol. 6 (Tokyo: Meiji Shoin, 1973–76).

Kaneyoshi (1402–81), whom he accompanied on a visit to the estates of the Kitabatake clan in Ise; thereafter, Shōkō took up residence in the Chiekō-in in Hasedera. During the same period he took trips to Mino (1470), Suruga (1473), Ichijōdani in Echizen, and Kohama in Wakasa (1477). On each journey he was warmly greeted by provincial clans such as the Saitō, the Imagawa, and the Takeda, who invited him to participate in poetic gatherings. Likewise, when in the capital he participated in poetry sessions held by Ashikaga Yoshimi (1439–91), Shōgō-in Dōkyō (d. 1501), Shiba Yoshikado (d. 1480?), Isshiki Yoshinao (d. 1483), Hatakeyama Yoshinari (d. 1490?), Ōuchi Masahiro (1446–95), and others. In all of this, however, he remained a poet-monk tossed on the waves of his age. As one scholar puts it, "This was a painful time—with his master gone, and he himself buffeted by the tides of war."[2]

In 1479 at the age of sixty-eight, Shōkō moved to Konkōji in Kitanoshō, Sakai, settling down in a *sōan,* or "grass hut." In 1480, 1481, and from the winter of 1482 to the spring of 1486, he was in Noto, receiving the patronage of Hatakeyama Yoshinari. Thereafter, until his death in 1493 at age eighty-two, he was active in Settsu and the area around the capital, living in his hermitage at Kitanoshō except for brief periods when he traveled to Echizen and Tango. His personal anthology for the last period of his life proceeds in diary style, and also offers detailed *kotobagaki,* or "prose prefaces," that give us a glimpse of one side of life in Sakai and the nearby estates of the Ikeda clan.

It was during the mid-sixteenth century that the city of Sakai in Izumi Province (modern day Osaka) gained prominence as one of the country's most rapidly developing regions in economic and cultural terms, a place that even Oda Nobunaga (1534–82) and Toyotomi Hideyoshi (1536–98) took pains to control. For that reason Sakai has attracted the attention of scholars, who have been able to create an image of the place through glimpses from a number of records of that time. Yet if we go back just a half century or so, to the beginning of the Sengoku period (ca. 1480), we find few historical sources to tell us about Sakai.

Shōkō's personal poetry collection, however, includes over 150 references to places and people located in Sakai, giving us an idea

2. Inada Toshinori, "Shōkō no denki ni kansuru shomondai," *Kokugo to kokubungaku* (July 1970).

of the poetic life of the area in the late fifteenth and early sixteenth centuries. The first reference he makes to the city dates from the autumn of the eleventh year of the Bunmei era (1479):

> (1) In the autumn of Bunmei 11, I turned the Chiekō-in over to someone else's care and took up life in vacant chambers located in the precincts of Amidōjō Konkōji in Kitanoshō, Sakai, Izumi Province.

Another record indicates that in fact Shōkō had some relationship with Sakai as early as Bunmei 7 (1475), before he moved there from the Chiekō-in.[3] It was in 1479, however, that he began residence there in the Amidōjō Konkōji, a temple of the Time sect (Ji shū).

Toward the end of the seventh month of Bunmei 12 (1480), Shōkō was invited to Noto by the shogunal constable (*shugo*) of that province, Hatakeyama Yoshinari, and stayed on there until the next spring. After this he stayed for a year around Kyoto. The next entry in his personal anthology relating to Sakai dates from the autumn of Bunmei 14 (1482):

> (2) Around the end of the seventh month, I went down to Sakai, where I stayed in quarters of the Amidōjō, and composed this poem, when people came over and started a round of poems.

In the tenth month of that same year, Shōkō went again to Noto, where he stayed for two periods that covered most of the next four years. However, references in *Shōken nichiroku* ("Shōken's Journal"), a diary kept by a Zen monk named Kikō Daishuku (1421–87), who himself had come to Sakai's Kaikaiji in the fifteenth year of the Bunmei era (1483) after a career at Tōfukuji in the capital, show that Shōkō was not forgotten even in his absence.[4] By then the poet seems to have been considered a resident of the place.

Shōkashū tells us that Shōkō left Noto in the summer of Bunmei 18 (1486), traveling to Echizen, Omi, and Miidera, and arriving in the capital on the twenty-second day of the sixth month of that

3. The other work is *Shōkō eiga*. Text is available in *Shikashū taisei*, vol. 6.
4. Shōken was one of Kikō Daishuku's other names. A printed text of his journal is available in the series *Dainihon kokiroku* (Tokyo: Iwanami Shoten, 1952–92).

same year. In the eighth month, he returned to Sakai, as is indicated by an entry in the anthology that records a poem written at Injōji.

> (3) In the eighth month, I came to Sakai in Izumi Province. On the night of the fifteenth, at Injōji, I wrote this poem on the topic "The Moon on the Night of the Fifteenth":
>
> For my lord, a gem
> offered up as a gift
> by a dragon—
> the moon midway through the month,
> afloat in the autumn night.
>
> kimi ga tame / ryū no sasaguru / tama ya kore /
> monaka ni ukabu / aki no yo no tsuki

Like Konkōji, Injōji was a temple of the Time sect. Later entries show that it would become the site of more poetry meetings involving Shōkō than any other place in Sakai. That two such temples would be so important to the poet's activities is testimony to the strong relationship between the Time sect and the arts in the medieval age.[5]

It is worth noting that the monk Kikō also quotes Shōkō's poem on the moon "afloat in the autumn night" in his *Shōken nichiroku* entry for the seventeenth day of the eighth month of Bunmei 18, noting it as a poem by Seiun—another of Shōkō's pseudonyms—from a poem contest held at Injōji. Evidently by this time the people of Sakai were developing regard for Shōkō's work.

Responding to that respect, Shōkō became more and more involved in the poetic affairs of the area, as these entries from Bunmei 18 (1486) show.

> (4) 8.23: From a three-poem contest held by Fujiwara Tomosuga.
> (5) 8.26: From a session (*ichiza*) at Injōji.
> (6) 9.10: From a contest among people at Eishōji.
> (7) From a fifty-poem sequence, around the same time, at the same temple.
> (8) From a session held by Fujiwara Toyonori.

5. For a study of the importance of the Time sect in medieval cultural affairs, see Kawai Kiyomitsu, *Ji shū bungei to Ippen Hōgo* (Tokyo: Tokyo Bijutsu, 1987).

At the beginning of the tenth month, Shōkō headed for Kawachi and was away from Sakai for twenty days or so, as is clear from his anthology and from a passage in *Shōken nichiroku* that says the monk Kikō sent one Kunsha "to call on the poet Seiun, but found him not at home." Then, on the seventeenth day of that same month, Kikō records this:

> Kitanosato destroyed by fire; one hundred buildings reduced to ash in an instant. Amidōjō burnt down, and also Kōjō-an inside. Nothing survived.

While Shōkō was away, a fire had broken out at Kitanosato—in other words, Kitanoshō—destroying Kōjō-an in Konkōji and reducing one hundred buildings to scorched earth. Perhaps because a fire was not the sort of thing to write a poem about, *Shōkashū* makes no mention of the incident, even in its prefaces. But the following prefaces indicate that Shōkō's quarters in Konkōji must have been unscathed.

(9) 10.24: I returned to my hut in Sakai and composed this for a round of poems held by Fujiwara Iesada.
(10) 11.5: From a round of poems held by Michihisa.
(11) Around the twelfth month: A young monk from Kaikaiji sketched plum trees on a fan, to which the priest Kikō added a Chinese poem. . . . I was asked to write a poem for the back of the fan, which featured a sketch of Ashiya village, and I obliged with this [poem], feeling it impossible to refuse.

This last entry is also the only mention of Kikō anywhere in *Shōkashū*. Happily, it is corroborated in *Shōken nichiroku,* which records the same poem by Shōkō, although it has a different one by Kikō himself. Kikō's diary ends on the last day of Bunmei 18 (corresponding to 24 January 1487). He died at Kaikaiji the following year, on the seventh day of the eighth month. Shōkō's anthology, however, goes on, listing 140 more entries involving Sakai and revealing the extent of his activities there in great detail. Below are a few representative entries that indicate his growing importance as an artist in the Sakai community.

1487

(12) 1.1: Written at my hut in Sakai, Izumi Province.
(13) 1.2: Written for a session, when some people came to my hut.

(14) 1.13: From a session at Injōji.
(15) 1.19: From a round of poems held by Sōchin.
(16) 2.4: Requested by Fujiwara Yasumasa.
(17) 2.12: Requested by Taira Tadanaga.
(18) 2.16: Requested by Sōchin.
(19) 3.6: From a session held under the blossoms at Shōrinji in Minaminoshō.
(20) 3.10: For a poem contest at Injōji.
(21) 3.14: Requested by Saeki Tadakane.
(22) At the end of the third month: From a session held when some people came to my hut.
(23) Around the end of the third month: Written when asked to judge a hundred-poem sequence written by the Awa lay monk Hosokawa Jōtai, of Izumi Province.
(24) 4.11: From among poems requested by Fujiwara Sadasuke.
(25) 4.22: From a session at the place of the monk Shingen, when the monk of Jōzen Konraiji was there.
(26) 5.15: From a round of poems held by Fujiwara Morishige.
(27) 5.20: From a round of poems composed at my hut.
(28) 5.26: Requested by Fujiwara Masatsugu.
(29) 6.10: From a three-poem contest at Injōji.
(30) 6.25: Requested by Fujiwara Tomokiyo.
(31) 8.10: From a three-poem contest at Injōji.
(32) 12.10: From a three-poem contest at Injōji.
(33) 12.23: From a session held by Fujiwara Tomokiyo.

1488

(34) 2.27: Written at Tanna's quarters at Injōji.
(35) 3.3: Some people invited me to go see high tide along the bay; on the way back we stopped at the home of a man named Kanjō and had a round of poems.
(36) 3.11: From a three-poem contest held by Fujiwara Iesada.
(37) 3.22: From the monthly three-poem contest at Injōji.
(38) 5.13: From a poem contest at Injōji.
(39) 5.29: When Nichi'en, chief monk of Honkokuji, came down to visit Jōjuji, a subtemple of Honkokuji, I went to see him. He gave me a poem strip (*tanzaku*) and asked me for a poem.
(40) I returned to my hut in Sakai on the twenty-third of the seventh month. On the night of the fifteenth, eighth month, some people came over and we had a session.
(41) 8.20: From the monthly gathering at my hut.
(42) 10.6: Written when a request was made for the poems composed at the monthly poem contest of the sixth month at Injōji.
(43) 10.14: Requested by Sōchin.
(44) On the twenty-fourth I returned to my hut. This was written on the twenty-seventh, when a man came and

told me that the period of the poem contest for the eighth month had been extended.

(45) 11.7: From among the poems to be critiqued at the monthly poetry gathering at Injōji.

(46) 11.28: From among the poems to be critiqued at the monthly poetry meeting at my hut.

(47) From the monthly poem contest at Injōji.

1489

(48) 1.8: Written for my monthly poetry meeting, at my hut.

(49) 1.10: From a sequence of thirty-six poems composed at a meeting at Injōji.

(50) 2.4: From the monthly poem contest at Injōji.

(51) On the twenty-ninth of the third month, I traveled to Ikeda and then on down to Sakai. This was composed for the monthly poem contest held at Injōji on the tenth of the fourth month.

(52) 4.13: From a session sponsored by Seijō, a new priest of the Jōrakuji.

(53) 5.10: From the monthly poem contest at Injōji.

(54) 5.14: Composed for a session held the first time I visited the home of Honjō Dannojō Saemon-no-jō Tadamasa.

(55) 5.20: From a round of poems composed when Fujiwara Yasumasa invited the monk of Injōji to his home.

(56) 7.3: From a session held by Dannojō Saemon-no-jō Fujiwara Tadamasa.

(57) 7.7: From a session held at Injōji.

(58) 7.10: From a poem contest at Injōji.

(59) 7.28: Written upon request as one of seven *waka* on the Holy Name prepared on the occasion of a visit to the home of Matsui Daijin-no-shō, who had just lost his two-year-old son.

(60) After I returned to my hut in Sakai on the sixth day of the tenth month, I composed this at the monthly meeting at Injōji on the twenty-seventh.

(61) 11.10: From the monthly poem contest at Injōji.

(62) 12.15: From a round of poems composed at Injōji for a dedicatory offering to Sumiyoshi Shrine

1490

(63) 1.10: From a fifty-poem sequence composed for the first monthly meeting of the new year at Injōji.

(64) 1.11: From a three-poem contest held for the first monthly poetry gathering of the year at Jōrakuji.

(65) 2.11: From the monthly poem contest at Jōrakuji.

(66) 2.12: From a ten-poem sequence composed at Ryūchin's hut.

(67) 2.20: From a three-poem contest at Injōji.

(68) 3.10: From the monthly poem contest at Injōji.

(69) 3.24: From the regular poem contest at Jōrakuji.
(70) 4.10: From the regular poem contest at Injōji.
(71) 4.11: From the regular poem contest at Jōrakuji.
(72) 4.12: From a round of twenty poems composed at the hut of Ryūchin.
(73) 4.30: From a round of twenty poems composed for a meeting held by Fujiwara Tadamasa.
(74) 5.8: From the regular poem contest at Jōrakuji.
(75) 5.10: From the regular poem contest at Injōji.
(76) 9.12: From a hundred-poem sequence written when Fujiwara Masatsugu was preparing to make a religious offering of poem papers (*kaishi*) in the hands of Teika and Ietaka, adorned with paintings on front and back.
(77) While on a trip through Bōshū and Kyushu, I had scattered poems here and there. In the autumn of Entoku 2 [1490], a man, called the lay monk Tadayoshi Shurinosuke of Hyūga, showed up at my hut in Sakai, Izumi Province, bringing with him a few of my poems that he had jotted down. At that time I wrote this poem.
(78) 10.9: From a three-poem contest, held after I had been away in the country and the monthly poem contest at Jōrakuji had not been held.
(79) 10.10: From a three-poem contest held to start up the monthly poetry meetings at Injōji again.
(80) 10.25: Fujiwara Tadamasa held a seven-day votive retreat at the shrine to the god of poetry, affiliated with Jōrakuji. Composed for poems on the same topics [as above].
(81) 10.27: From among a round of thirty poems written when I invited Fujiwara Tadamasa to visit me after I moved to the hut by the entrance to the temple.
(82) 11.3: From a session held when the monk of Injōji came to my hut.
(83) 11.8: From the regular poem contest at Jōrakuji.
(84) 11.9: From a group of twenty-five poems written for criticism at a session held when the head monk of Konkōji invited the monk of Injōji to visit.
(85) 11.10: From the monthly poem contest at Injōji.
(86) 11.11: From a poem contest at the Tsūgen-an.
(87) 11.12: From a session held when some people came to my hut.
(88) 11.14: From a group of poems written for criticism at a session held at the quarters of Kakua in Konkōji.
(89) 11.16: From a session held the first time I visited the residence of Saeki Yoshitsugu.
(90) 12.4: From a round of twenty poems written when I called over the holy men of Jōrakuji.
(91) 12.9: From the monthly poem contest at Jōrakuji.

(92) 12.10: From the regular monthly poem contest at Injōji.
(93) 12.27: Written on the twenty-seventh of the same month, when I returned to my hut in Sakai.

1491

(94) 1.5: For a one-poem *kaishi* written for the first monthly meeting of the new year at Tsūgen-an.
(95) 1.6: From a round of fifteen poems composed at the residence of Fujiwara Tadamasa.
(96) 1.10: For a one-poem *kaishi* written for the first monthly meeting of the new year at Injōji.
(97) 1.11: After Taira Matajirō Tokitomo asked me to mark a hundred-poem sequence, he sent me a colored-shell vial of perfume, and I sent this in return.
(98) 1.18: From a monthly poem contest at Tsūgen-an.
(99) 1.20: From a three-poem contest at the monthly meeting at Konkōji.
(100) 1.20: From a session held by Sōchin.
(101) 1.21: From among twenty poems composed when I first visited the residence of Fujiwara Kanechika.
(102) 1.28: From a fifty-poem sequence sponsored by Saeki Tadakane.
(103) Second month: I returned from Ibaraki on the fourth and composed this on the eighth, for a poem contest held at Tsūgen-an.
(104) 2.17: Written upon request when the monthly poem contest at Injōji had been postponed.
(105) 4.10: From the monthly poem contest at Injōji.
(106) 4.27: From the monthly poem contest at Jōrakuji.
(107) 6.16: Fujiwara Iesada passed away last month, on the twelfth. His Buddhist name is Sōgon. This poem is from a round of thirty composed in his memory, on the fifty-seventh day since his death.
(108) 6.20: From a monthly poem contest at Jōrakuji, held when a request had been made for the poems of the fifth month.
(109) 6.25: From a monthly poem contest at Konkōji, upon request for a copy of the poems of the fifth month.
(110) 8.15: From a three-poem contest held by Fujiwara Kanechika at a place called Keiun-an.
(111) From the same time, composed for a round of thirty poems on the fifteenth night of the month.
(112) 8.16: From a session held by Fujiwara Hisa[sic] in the quarters of a temple called Amidaji.
(113) From a session sponsored by Fujiwara Yoshiakira.
(114) 8.20: From a round of fifty poems held at the Keiun-an.
(115) 8.22: Written when there was a request for poems from the poem contest of the seventh month at Konkōji.
(116) 8.23: From the monthly poem contest at Jōrakuji.

(117) 9.10: From the monthly poem contest at Tsūgen-an.
(118) 9.15: From a sequence of fifteen poems requested by Fujiwara Masatsugu.
(119) 9.16: From a dedicatory sequence requested by Saeki Tadakane for presentation at Sumiyoshi Shrine.
(120) 9.23: On "Waiting for the Moon," from a session held by Fujiwara Munekura.
(121) 9.24: From the monthly poem contest at Tsūgen-an.
(122) [Tenth month] From a sequence of fifty poems requested by some people at a session held at Konkōji.
(123) 10.9: At the regular monthly poem contest at Tsūgen-an.
(124) 11.6: From a twenty-poem sequence for criticism held by Sōchin.
(125) 11.15: From a three-poem sequence at the hut of Ryūchin.
(126) 11.20: From the monthly poem contest at Konkōji.
(127) 11.25: From the monthly poem contest at Tsūgen-an.
(128) 11.28: From a three-poem contest held by Jōzen at the abbot's quarters (*tatchū*) of Zentsūji.
(129) [Twelfth month] On the eleventh of that same month, I returned to my hut in Sakai. On the twenty-second I wrote this poem, from a group of three produced for criticism at Tsūgen-an.
(130) 12.25: From a three-poem contest held at the monthly meeting at the same temple.

1492

(131) 1.6: A one-poem *kaishi* for the first monthly meeting of the new year at Tsūgen-an.
(132) 1.8: From a fifteen-poem sequence composed at the residence of Dannojō Saemon-no-jō Taira Tadamasa.
(133) 1.12: People were making the rounds, discussing poems in a contest. Because it was still quite cold, they went everywhere. This poem is from a session held at my hut.
(134) 2.17: From a round of poems composed at the residence of Fujiwara Kanechika.
(135) 2.25: From a monthly three-poem contest at Tsūgen-an.
(136) End of the third month: From a ten-poem sequence *extempore* requested by Saeki Tadakane.
(137) 5.20: Written at a sutra service on the fifty-seventh day after the death of Tōbō Hōin Chinsei of Jōrakuji.
(138) 5.22: Requested by Fujiwara Mitsutada.
(139) 6.24: Written for a six-poem contest sponsored by Sōchin.
(140) 8.11: From a three-poem contest held by Kasai Tōgorō at the residence of Fujiwara Mototsuna.
(141) 9.25: From a three-poem contest at Tsūgen-an.
(142) 11.18: From a poem contest at Tsūgen-an.
(143) 11.21: Written at a three-poem contest sponsored by Fujiwara Tsuneharu.
(144) 12.18: From a three-poem contest at Tsūgen-an.

1493

(145) 1.6: From the regular monthly meeting at Tsūgen-an.

(146) From a fifty-poem sequence produced spontaneously at the same session.

(147) 1.18: From among poems written to be critiqued at a poem contest.

(148) 1.19: Written when people got together in one of the dormitories of Jōrakuji.

(149) 1.30: From among thirty poems composed at Sōchin's.

(150) 2.10: From a round of poems written at the home of Deputy Kosaka, in the administrative office of South Sakai, when I was invited by the monk of Injōji.

(151) 3.17: Written when I returned to my hut in Sakai.

(152) 4.2: Written when a session was held with poets and connoisseurs at the Baichū-bō in Jōrakuji, which was being used as a dormitory by the Ouchi Suō Gon-no-suke, then in the Kawachi campaign.

(153) 4.6: Written at a banquet when I was asked for a poem by Uragami Norimune, governor of Mimasaka—then encamped nearby in connection with a campaign—who was visiting a hut on the grounds of the Shōhōji in Sakai, Izumi Province.

(154) 4.9: From a session held by Norimune, governor of Mimasaka, at Shōhōji.

These entries from Shōkō's personal anthology show the extent of his contacts with the people of the Sakai area, to whom he seems to have been a teacher and arbiter of taste, as well as a source of well-written poems for ceremonial and other formal occasions. A short summary of what is known about the places and men he mentions will tell us a good deal about the poetic society of the city in the late fifteenth century.

Places

(1) After Injōji, the place most often mentioned in Shōkō's prefaces is Jōrakuji, a temple founded by Ennin (794–864) in 852. Associated with it was a Tenman Shrine, which honored a wooden statue of the great Sugawara Michizane (845–903), the patron-god of poets, who had traveled through the area. It was at this shrine that Fujiwara Tadamasa spent seven days in ritual seclusion during the tenth month of Entoku 2 (1490; see 80 above). Nothing is known, however, about the Baichū-bō mentioned as the place where the Ōuchi encamped in Meiō 2 (1493; see 152 above).

(2) Kaikaiji, where the monk Kikō had his residence, was a cloister of the Rinzai School of Zen. Until the fire of the Genna era, it was located just outside the west gate of what is now Akuchi Shrine. At present it is inside the precincts of Nanshūji.

(3) Shōrinji was also a temple of the Rinzai School of Zen. It still survives in eastern Shōrinji-chō. In the past its precincts were said to reach over the present Shōrinji-chō to the coast.

(4) Jōjuji was a subtemple of Kyoto's Honkokuji, of the Nichiren sect. Later, at the time of the Hokke Uprising in Tenbun 5 (1536), it was used as the temporary headquarters of Honkokuji, explaining why it is still today called Rokujō. It is located in eastern Shukuya-chō.

(5) Amidaji is probably a reference to Ōamidakyōdera, referred to as Kyokurensha. It is a temple of the Pure Land sect. It survives in Teraji-chō Higashi.

(6) Zentsūji was a temple of the Rinzai School of Zen. It was incorporated into Shōrinji in Meiji 39 (1906).

(7) Shōhōji was likewise a temple of the Pure Land sect; it still survives in eastern Nakano-chō. It was here that Uragami Norimune (1429–1502) encamped his soldiers in the fourth month of Meiō 2 (1493; see 152–53 above). During the second month of that year, the shogun Ashikaga Yoshiki (otherwise known as Yoshitane; 1466–1523), went to the aid of Hatakeyama Masanaga (d. 1493) and attacked Hatakeyama Motoie. In response, Ōuchi Yoshioki (1477–1528), Uragami Norimune, and other generals moved troops into Kawachi and the Sakai area (because the latter was a place with many temples and thus well suited for an encampment). That the generals in this case invited poets to their chambers between skirmishes and held poetry gatherings is reminiscent of the scene in *Taiheiki* ("The Great Peace") in which the shogun invited *rengashi* over and began a ten-thousand-verse *renga* sequence under the blossoms while surrounding Chihaya Castle.[6]

People

The men mentioned by Shōkō about whom the most is known are, not surprisingly, both poets. The first is Sōchin, about whom the *rengashi* Shōhaku, another resident of the Sakai area, makes this

6. See Helen Craig McCullough, trans., *The Taiheiki: A Chronicle of Medieval Japan* (New York: Columbia University Press, 1959), 184–85.

comment in his personal poetry anthology, *Shunmusō* ("Jottings from a Spring Dream")[7]:

> I heard that the monk Sōchin has passed away. He was a man of sensitivity whom I had known many years, and the news brings tears of sadness to my eyes. He was a man who put his soul into the way of poetry, one who had written more than twenty copies of *Genji monogatari*—a task that seems to me unparalleled. Furthermore, he never rested from his study of poetic works. But recently he fell ill, and now he is gone. When I learned that until the very end he was writing a copy of Genji—passing away when he had reached the "Morning Glory" chapter—it made my grief more intense.
>
> His was a pledge
> cherished long in his heart,
> set down by his brush
> as he faded away
> like dew on the morning glory.
>
> fude ni some / kokoro ni kakeshi / chigiri to ya /
> orishi mo kieshi / asagao no tsuyu

Although not dated, this entry indicates that Sōchin died about the time Shōhaku's anthology was compiled, in Eishō 15 (1518). And another source identifies Sōchin as "a *rengashi* of Sakai."

> Sōchin: disciple of Shōhaku; named Bandōya. Died while copying the "Morning Glory" chapter of *Genji*.

That Sōchin is remembered here as Bandōya, literally "tradesman of the East Slope,"[8] is of interest considering the importance of commercial development in Sakai, especially so given what we know about Shōhaku's own interactions with people of the merchant class in that same area.[9]

7. The text is available in *Shikashū taisei,* vol. 6. The headnote precedes poem 2142.
8. The precise meaning of *bandōya* is unclear. It may mean that Sōchin came from the Kantō, "east of the gate"; it is probable, in any case, that he had commercial connections, given his residence in Sakai.
9. Shōhaku moved to Ina in Settsu Province at the time of the Ōnin War and later on moved to Sakai itself, where he acted as a teacher to amateur poets of that commercial area.

The other relatively well known poet mentioned by Shōkō is the monk Kakua (see 88 above). He too is identified in Shōhaku's *Shunmusō,* albeit only in a headnote that mentions the monk as living in "Konkōji, Sakai, Izumi Province." Since Shōhaku's entry was written around 1515–18, there is a gap of thirty years between the mention of Kakua in Shōkō's anthology and the one in Shōhaku's. An active linked-verse poet involved in a number of documented *renga* sequences, Kakua was evidently a student of Shōhaku's in those later years.

Thus, other sources place some of Shōkō's poetic companions in Sakai at appropriate times and give us some hints about their backgrounds. Such information on many of the other people mentioned in Shōkō's anthology is scarce. What little is known shows us that many of them were of the warrior class. Honjō Tadamasa, for instance, is called by the clan name Fujiwara in one place (56), and Taira in another (132). Beyond this, one document of the time seems to indicate that the Honjō family held the office of deputy (*daikan*) for the Kitanoshō in Sakai. Whatever the case, it is clear that Honjō Dannojō Saemon Tadamasa was a powerful warrior of the Sakai area. The same is probably true of Hosokawa Tsuneyasu (see 23 above), who is probably of the same family as Hosokawa Tsuneari, *shugo* of Izumi Province.

One of the most interesting figures mentioned by Shōkō, however, is one of the last, the man named Kosaka of the administrative office (*mandokoro*) of South Sakai, who is probably identifiable with one Kosaka Jirō Saemonnojō Yasuhide, deputy of Sakai's Minaminoshō. A document in the collection of the Kaikō Shrine makes it clear that, when a dispute over money involving shrines affiliated with Nenbutsuji and Sumiyoshi Shrine occurred in Meiō 2 (1493), it was Kosaka Yasuhide, deputy of Minaminoshō, who was called in to arbitrate the matter, deciding things in favor of Nenbutsuji in 1493. Moreover, a similar complaint was sent to none other than Honjō Motoie, a representative of the Honjō clan mentioned earlier in relation to Shōkō. Thus, in the year of Shōkō's death an example exists of financial control being carried out directly by *nayashū,* powerful "warehousemen," half a century before Sakai is usually said to have become a "free city" in economic terms. The Honjō and Kosaka families had charge over Kitanoshō and Minaminoshō, and they directly handled all complaints. Perhaps, then, when the monk of Injōji invited Shōkō to accompany him to the residence of the administrative offices of South Sakai, he may have realized that getting acquainted with the Kosaka—even through a poetry gathering—would be of some advantage in the future.

In these meetings with people of Sakai, Shōkō of course played the role of leader in matters of poetry. He acted as lector, he sometimes provided criticism (see 45, 46, 84, 88, 124, 129, 147), and he occasionally was asked to "mark" other's work (23 and 97). Further proof that he was the central figure in poetic circles at the time is provided by entries 78 and 79, which show that while he was away from his hermitage (traveling to Kyoto, Wakasa, Tango, then through Ikeda and back home) the monthly poetry meetings held at Jōrakuji and Injōji were discontinued for four or five months. Only after his return did the meetings resume on a regular basis.

The particular kind of poetic composition that is most often seen in Shōkō's anthology is the *tsugiuta,* or "round of poems," a popular form of the time that involved folding papers into three parts, writing topics down and concealing them behind folds, and then passing the topics out for each participant to compose an appropriate verse on the spot. This kind of poetry may be inferior to linked verse—then in its heyday—as a "communal" form of art. In linked verse the participants in a session took turns composing shorter and longer verses to make up a complete whole in fifty or one hundred verses; in the *tsugiuta,* however, each poet created his own complete poem rather than one communally produced work. But, since it involved poets meeting together in one session, in the same place, the latter form was also appropriate to the medieval "communal" ethos. In the case of the gatherings in Sakai, the atmosphere would not have been as sedate and formal as in similar meetings at the court or in the homes of the nobility; instead, the poetic meetings led by Shōkō brought together close friends of similar social status.

It is also worth noting that men like Kakua and Sōchin, both major figures in the poetic world of Sakai who in the early sixteenth century became central figures in the world of *renga,* received some of their first instruction back in Sakai, in meetings where criticism was offered by Shōkō.

Judging from available records, "tradesmen" such as Kakua of Konkōji and Sōchin were probably men of business. In addition, the monk Kikō and the priests Ryūchin and Sōkan also appear in the pages of *Shōkashū*; but most of the other people mentioned appear to be of the warrior class, beginning with deputies such as Honjō Tadamasa and Kosaka Yasuhide of the Kitanoshō and Minaminoshō in Sakai, and going on to include those who called themselves Fujiwara. These people were the warriors and *kokujin* ("men of the provinces," who acted as semi-independent owners of property) who lived in and around the Sakai area.

Most studies of Sakai have said little about the warrior classes there, concentrating instead on the activities of merchants. But in the Muromachi and Sengoku periods it was the warrior class that had a greater impact on literary culture, particularly so in the case of *uta* and *renga*. The travel records of Sōgi (1421–1502), Sōchō (1448–1532), and Sōboku (d. 1545) show in great detail how much material and financial support they received from provincial warriors. And Shōkō, too, after settling down in Sakai, still traveled to the provinces occasionally with the support of such *shugo daimyō* as the Hatakeyama in Noto, the Isshiki in Tango, and the Asakura in Echizen. In Settsu Ikeda, he was in fact so favored by the patronage of the *kokujin* Ikeda family that he had a home there, called the Seiun-an.

Thus, Shōkō looked to powerful provincial lords as patrons, and even in Sakai he had a number of patrons from the military ranks. In the poetry gatherings of Sakai, however, there was a difference, as a few references to the above-mentioned Ikeda family of Settsu make clear.

Shōkō's first recorded meeting with Ikeda Masatane, governor of Wakasa, occurred in the spring of Bunmei 14 (1482), as noted in the following entry from *Shōkashū*:

> In the spring of that same year [1482], a message came telling me that Sōgi and the lay monk Sugihara Sōi of Iga were at the residence of Masatane, governor of Wakasa, in Settsu Ikeda, and asking me if I would like to come up too. I made the trip and composed three poems when people had a poem contest there, of which this is one.

What first attracts interest here is that Shōkō was invited to Ikeda by the *renga* masters Sōgi and Sōi (1418–85), who later were involved in a linked-verse session at the same time, although Shōkō was not. But this is the first time that his presence can be verified in Ikeda.

Five years later, in Chōkyō 1 (1487), Shōkō was in Ikeda again, and then again three times the next year. For one of these visits, the poet gives this information, reminiscent of entry 59 above:

> Chōkyō 2.7.9: A messenger came from the governor of Wakasa in Ikeda, asking for thirty-six Buddhist Holy Name poems during the time of intermediate existence for Hikojirō Masamasa, who had died on the second. This is one of the poems.

In addition to these entries, there are twelve more referring to various members of the Ikeda family in Shōkō's anthology, the last appearing on the third month of Meiō 2 (1493), the year of the poet's death. During that time, Shōkō developed a classic patron-client relationship with Masatane and his family, participating in poetry contests in Ikeda, providing dedicatory verses for special occasions, and in general acting the part of a teacher for his warrior patron. That he was asked to provide appropriate poems upon the deaths of two Ikeda family members—the one noted above and another in 1490—shows that he was also highly esteemed by the family.

Yet it is significant that in his travels to Settsu, Shōkō only seems to have developed relationships with the high-ranking members of the Ikeda family. And this is true of his relations with the warriors of Noto as well, where he met only with Hatakeyama Yoshinari and the latter's more senior retainers. Furthermore, this same situation can be seen in his relations with the Ōuchi of Suō. In his dealings with provincial warriors, Shōkō limited himself, or was limited by circumstance, to contact with only the elite of warrior society.

In his activities in Sakai, however, there is no such trend. There poetic gatherings were not only for certain authority figures but for a variety of people, including the Honjō family, the Kosaka family, and others. Although there is no record of all participants in these meetings as there is for some *renga* sessions, it appears that whereas among powerful *kokujin* of other areas the *ichiza*, or "session," was made up of people decided by feudal ties and rank, among the people of Sakai the group was made up of people who simply lived in the same area.

The special features of the poetry meetings of warriors in Sakai were thus intimately connected to the political and economic situation of the early Sengoku period. For Sakai was at the time neither a territory under direct shogunal control, nor a place under the firm control of a *kokujin* lord of independent spirit. Instead, in that area *kokujin* lords of similar strength formed a group loosely centered on the deputies of Kitanoshō and Minaminoshō. And since no single person was in a position of authority, the group was an open one. All of this is, in my opinion, reflected in their poetry meetings. The era of the independent *nayashū* was approaching fast, with the glory of the Azuchi-Momoyama period showing itself when Sakai was supposedly still under direct shogunal control.

Sōgi and the Imperial House

Kaneko Kinjirō
Translated by H. Mack Horton

The history of the relationship between the *renga* master Sōgi (1421–1502) and the imperial house during the reign of Emperor Go-Tsuchimikado (1442–1500; r. 1464–1500) can be traced with the aid of extant documents dating from 1474, near the end of the Ōnin War (1467–77), to 1499, the year before Sōgi left for Echigo on his last journey. Sōgi had spent the earlier years of the Ōnin conflict in the Kantō area, but by 1473 he had returned to the capital and made it the center of his poetic activity. For much of the first half of the next quarter century, Sōgi was engaged in travel to such far-removed provinces as Echigo and Yamaguchi, and his interaction with the emperor was infrequent. But their contact increased during the final decade, particularly in and after 1495, the year *Shinsen tsukubashū* ("New Tsukuba Collection"), the second imperially recognized anthology of linked verse, was compiled.

Extant records show their dealings with each other to have consisted largely of requests from the emperor for direction in the composition of linked verse, with imperial patronage for Sōgi in return. That patronage, however, was of an intangible, spiritual nature and did not involve overt political or financial advantage. The following discussion will begin by considering the strong attraction to linked verse on the part of the imperial house.[1] It will then trace the

1. Morozumi Sōichi, "Saiseiki no dōjō rengadan," *Renga haikai kenkyū* 16 (July 1958); "Go-Tsuchimidadotei rengadan no sakuhin ni tsuite," *Yamanashi Kenritsu Joshi Daigaku kiyō* 3 (March 1969); and Watanuki Toyoaki, "Go-Tsuchimikadotei rengadan to Shōhaku," *Chūō Daigaku Daigaku'in kenkyū nenpyō, bungaku kenkyūka hen* (March 1984).

gradual deepening of Sōgi's relationship with the emperor, the nature of his linked-verse tutelage, and finally the close cooperation between the two men during work on *Shinsen tsukubashū*.[2]

Linked Verse and the Go-Tsuchimikado Court

The avid composition of linked verse by Emperor Go-Tsuchimikado, Crown Prince Katsuhito (who later became Emperor Go-Kashiwabara, 1464–1526; r. 1500–26), and the courtiers in their service no doubt included an element of escapism, occurring as it did at the height of the Ōnin War. But in light of the frequency of their sessions for the composition of *uta, renga,* and *wakan renku* (linked verse in Japanese and Chinese), and the importance this activity played in their daily lives, it seems likely that their fervor represented as much an artistic decision to live through poetry as to escape through it. This attitude was reinforced by the long commitment to literature on the part of the princely Fushiminomiya house, Go-Tsuchimikado's ancestors. His father, Go-Hanazono (1419–71; r. 1428–64) was the son of Fushiminomiya Sadafusa (Go-Sukō'in; 1372–1456), a dedicated scholar whose works included a forty-four-fascicle diary in Chinese (*kanbun*) entitled *Kanmon gyoki* ("Journal of Things Seen and Heard"), an anthology of his own poetry named *Sagyoku wakashū* ("Jewels and Sand"), and *Chin'yōki* ("Camelia Leaves"), a treatise on the education of a sovereign that Sadafusa presented to his son Go-Hanazono on the latter's assumption of the throne.[3] Of these, *Kanmon gyoki* is especially well known for its wealth of information on political, social, and artistic life from 1416 to 1448. *Uta* and *renga* occur with particular frequency within its pages, and notes concerning *tsukinami renga,* monthly linked-verse meetings, appear year after

2. Ijichi Tetsuo, *Sōgi* (Tokyo: Seigodō, 1943); Kaneko Kinjirō, *Shinsen tsukubashū no kenkyū* (Tokyo: Kazama Shobō, 1969); and Uzawa Satoru, "*Sanetakakōki* ni arawaretaru kyūtei bungei," *Chiba Daigaku Bunrigakubu kiyō, bunka kagaku* 1.1 (1953).

3. A printed text of *Kanmon gyoki* is available in supplement 2 (2 vols.) of Hanawa Hokiichi and Hanawa Tadatomi, comps., *Zoku gunsho ruijū,* 3d rev. ed. (Tokyo: Zoku Gunsho Ruijū Kanseikai, 1974–75). *Sagyoku wakashū* appears in vol. 8 of *Shinpen kokka taikan* (Tokyo: Kadokawa Shoten, 1991). *Chin'yōki* can be found in Hanawa Hokiichi and Kawamata Keiichi, comps., *Shinkō gunsho ruijū,* vol. 2 (no. 30) (Tokyo: Meichō Fukyūkai, 1977–78).

year. Male as well as female *renga* specialists from outside the court, including Tōju, Zensui, and Shōyū (fl. 1430–40), the official Commissioner for *Renga* at Kitano Shrine (*Kitano kaisho renga bugyō*), were often invited to participate in these gatherings. Many pages of the linked verses composed there survive because Sadafusa kept his diary on their reverse sides.[4] His love of linked verse was passed on to his son Go-Hanazono and thence to Go-Tsuchimikado and Katsuhito. They too met with *renga* specialists from outside the court, although the exalted position of emperor made it impossible for them to interact in person with those not of courtier rank. That restriction did not apply to Sadafusa, who never took the throne himself.

Go-Hanazono abdicated in favor of his son Go-Tsuchimikado in 1464. With the outbreak of the Ōnin War in 1467, both took refuge in the Muromachi Palace of Shogun Ashikaga Yoshimasa (1436–90) on the thirteenth day of the eighth month. Go-Hanazono died there on the twenty-seventh of the twelfth month of Bunmei 2 (early 1471). During his years on the throne, he had presided over the compilation of the last imperial anthology of *waka* poetry, *Shin shokukokinshū* (1439), which included twelve of his own compositions. He also left a three-volume anthology of his own poetry, *Go-Hanazono'in gyoshū*, and his linked-verse compositions included a solo hundred-verse sequence, *Go-Hanazono'in godokugin hyakuin*. The work was a lament (*jukkai*) composed at Muromachi Palace in the twelfth month of the second year of Ōnin (early 1469). The severity of that winter is readily apparent in the first three verses:

Its branches grown old,
the pine is now crowned by
a cover of snow.

eda ni furinu / ima ya itadaku / yuki no matsu

Years having piled upon years,
we reach the depths of winter.

tsumoreru toshi wa / fuyu fukaki koro

4. Yajima Masaharu, "Go-Sukō'in eisō o megutte," *Shoryōbu kiyō* 31 (February 1977); Itō Kunio, "Fushiminomiya rengakai to *Genji* yoriai," *Kokubungaku kō* 81 (March 1979); and Kunaichō Shoryōbu, *Go-Sukō'in to Fushiminomiya-bon tenji mokuroku* (October 1984).

On my sleeping place
beams of bare and chilling light
are cast by the moon.[5]

toko no ue / kage susamashiku / tsuki sashite

The third page of the same sequence contains a pair of verses that appear to express the emperor's desires for peace and for his own return to the imperial palace:

The emperor now returns
to the Ninefold Enclosure.

kimi kokonoe ni / kaeru kono toki

The tumult of waves
around the thousand hamlets
are suddenly stilled.[6]

sawagitsuru / nami no chisato no / osamarite

But Go-Hanazono died with those hopes unfulfilled.

The deep attraction linked verse held for members of the Fushiminomiya line is also apparent in Go-Hanazono's epistle to his son Go-Tsuchimikado, *Go-Hanazono'in goshōsoku,* also known as *Tōgu ni okurasetamau onfumi* ("Letter Presented to the Crown Prince"). The letter was written in 1462, two years before the crown prince acceded to the throne at the age of twenty-two.[7] It consists of only seven sections plus an introduction and afterword, but despite its short length, two of the sections are devoted to *renga* and *wakan renku.* A third, an exhortation to scholarship, likewise includes passages on *uta, renga,* Chinese poetry, and *wakan renku.* The first section dealing with linked verse reads in full as follows:

> When a verse is composed, do not recklessly criticize it, no matter how poor the attempt. Since your own studies are not yet advanced, you must not ignore Lord

5. Text available in *Zoku gunsho ruijū,* vol. 17 (no. 482) (Tokyo: Zoku Gunsho Ruijū Kanseikai, 1974–75), 604.
6. Ibid., 605.
7. Hashimoto Yoshihiko, "Go-Hanazono'in goshōsoku," *Kokushi daijiten,* vol. 5 (Tokyo: Yoshikawa Kōbunkan, 1985), 957.

> Fushimi and myself and pronounce on the verses at a session. I repeat, at present you still lack experience. Adverse comments on verses that are in fact unobjectionable will embarrass only yourself.[8]

The content here is nearly identical to passages in works of *renga* theory that set forth the desirable mental attitude for poets at a linked-verse session. It also includes the term *sabaku,* commonly used at *renga* gatherings to mean the appraisal of each successive verse and the direction of the progress of a sequence. The interest of Go-Hanazono's advice lies not only in what it counsels with regard to mental attitude and deportment, but more particularly in what it implies about the young Go-Tsuchimikado's accustomed behavior at *renga* sessions. It was the youthful exuberance hinted at here that led to the intense *renga* of his mature years. The "Lord Fushimi" of the passage refers, if the date 1462 is correct, to Go-Hanazono's younger brother, Prince Sadatsune, heir to the Fushiminomiya house.

The section of the letter dealing with *wakan renku* encourages the crown prince to practice linking Japanese verses (*waku*) to preceding Japanese verses, rather than to focus on Chinese verses (*kanku*), which involve complex questions of interpretation. Go-Hanazono adds that his son must exercise particular caution in light of the recent participation of the courtier literatus Ichijō Kaneyoshi (1402–81) and the shogun, Ashikaga Yoshimasa. The counsel given in this second passage is elementary yet pertinent, especially with regard to the advisability of linking a second Japanese verse (*tsukeku*) to a Japanese *maeku.* It also includes advice on dealing with others at a poetry session.

In the section of the letter treating scholarship, Go-Hanazono urges his son to abandon the currently popular practice of collecting pet birds and to concentrate instead on his studies, in order that he might one day accede to the throne and rule with gentleness and benevolence. But the fact that here too the author returns to matters of *renga* and *wakan renku* shows how central such poetry was to daily life at court. The advice in this and the two preceding passages of the Go-Hanazono letter is an important point of reference when considering the subsequent poetic activity of his son.

8. *Shinkō gunsho ruijū,* vol. 6, 640.

Only two years after Go-Tsuchimikado became emperor, the Ōnin War began, and he was to spend the rest of his life enveloped in political and social turmoil. On the thirteenth day of the eleventh month, 1476, Yoshimasa's Muromachi Palace burned, and Go-Tsuchimikado took refuge in Kitanokōji-dono, the residence of Yoshimasa's mother. Three years later, on the first of the seventh month, 1479, that complex was razed as well, and the emperor found lodgings where he could until finally, on the seventh of the twelfth month (early 1480), he was able to return to his original residence, the Tsuchimikado Palace. Its buildings had been used by the enemy during the Ōnin conflict, and subsequent repairs had proceeded only sporadically. The emperor resided there until his death on the twenty-eighth of the ninth month, 1500, and the imperial treasury was at the time so depleted it is said that his funeral ceremony could not be held for more than forty days.

Go-Tsuchimikado thus spent his entire life beset by the unrest that led soon after to the national chaos of the Sengoku era, "The Age of the Country at War." He was nevertheless able to pursue poetry with great energy. *Uta* sessions were held even during his years at the Muromachi Palace, albeit on a reduced scale, and monthly palace poetry gatherings were formally reinaugurated not long after his return to the Tsuchimikado residence, probably in 1481.[9] The emperor himself compiled a number of personal poetry anthologies, among them *Kōjin kaishū* ("A Collection of Red Embers") and *Go-Tsuchimikado gyoshū* ("Emperor Go-Tsuchimikado's Collection").[10]

The passion for linked verse on the part of the Go-Tsuchimikado court can be traced through diaries and extant *renga* compositions, many of which have already been afforded scholarly investigation. They show that linked-verse meetings were rare, as might be expected, in and around the years of the Ōnin War, but that they gradually increased from 1472 onward, culminating in remarkable activity in the latter half of Go-Tsuchimikado's reign.

Sōgi returned to the *renga* world of the capital in 1473. In 1474 Palace Chamberlain Sanjōnishi Sanetaka (1455–1537) began keeping

9. For more information on *waka* composition in the court see Inoue Muneo, *Chūsei kadanshi no kenkyū, Muromachi zenki*, rev. ed. (Tokyo: Kazama Shobō, 1984).

10. These two collections are available in vol. 6 of *Shikashū taisei* (Tokyo: Meiji Shoin, 1973–76) and vol. 7 of *Shinpen kokka taikan*.

his diary *Sanetakakōki,* and in 1477 the female officials (*nyokan*) in the emperor's service began their collective palace record *Oyudono no ue nikki* ("Journal of the Imperial Bath Attendants").[11] Entries in both diaries pertaining to linked verse at the palace were made increasingly as the years progressed, but such meetings did not become truly frequent until after the emperor returned to the Tsuchimikado Palace in early 1480. Thereafter the number grew yearly. This palace activity centered on the emperor himself, but it also included gatherings sponsored by Crown Prince Katsuhito, which are mentioned as early as 1475. Both the emperor and the prince composed *renga* and *wakan renku,* a practice common to court society in general. The two types appear frequently in *Kanmon gyoki,* and both, as we have seen, are taken up in *Go-Hanazono'in goshōsoku.* In fact, *Wakan renku* seems to have been the preserve of the aristocracy and not much practiced by military houses or in the provinces.

Let us now examine the *renga* activity of Go-Tsuchimikado's court in greater detail. On the twenty-fifth of the first month, 1479, nearly a year before the return of the emperor to the Tsuchimikado Palace, monthly sessions were held to compose votive *renga* (*hōraku*) for Kitano Tenmangū Shrine, where Sugawara Michizane is venerated as the god of poetry and scholarship. Similar sessions were held without fail on the twenty-fifth day of each succeeding month as well. As an intercalary month fell after the ninth month of that year, a total of thirteen sessions were convened. Furthermore, thousand-verse (*senku*) votive *renga* were also composed in 1481, 1482, 1484, 1485, 1487, and 1490. Fourteen ninety-four, the year before the compilation of *Shinsen tsukubashū,* was particularly rich in *renga* activity at court and included the following events:

Monthly votive *renga* at the palace for Kitano Shrine (*Dairi Kitano hōraku tsukinami renga*)	11 times
Thousand-verse votive *renga* at the palace for Yoshida Shrine (*Dairi Yoshida hōraku senku renga*)	1 time
Palace *renga* (*Dairi renga*)	15 times

11. Text available as supplement 3 (11 vols.) to *Zoku gunsho ruijū.*

Palace one-hundred day *renga* (*Dairi hyakunichi renga*) from 9.1

Palace *wakan renku* (*Dairi wakan renku*) 20 times

Renga at the crown prince's quarters (*Shinnō onkata renga*) 12 times

The precise nature of the "palace one-hundred day *renga*" is unclear, but it very likely resembled another observance with the same name held in 1492 from the third of the third month. At that time, *renga* were composed each day through the thirteenth of the sixth month, for a total of six thousand verses. The purpose of the exercise was composition practice, and it consumed a large part of each day. At the same time, the usual *renga* and *wakan renku* gatherings at the palace and crown prince's quarters continued to be held, as well as the monthly and thousand-verse formal votive sequences. The extraordinary efflorescence of *renga* activity in the palace at that time continued unabated after the compilation of *Shinsen tsukubashū* (1495) and up until the death of Go-Tsuchimikado in 1500. *Shinsen tsukubashū* itself owes its existence in large part to the remarkable passion for *renga* at the palace during those years.

The number of *renga* works from Go-Tsuchimikado's court that survives is surprisingly large, considering the destructive nature of the times.[12] It includes two sequences of one thousand verses and seventy-one of one hundred verses. Even excluding *wakan renku* compositions, the number far exceeds that of any previous reign. The emperor and the crown prince were also well represented in *Shinsen tsukubashū*, the former with 108 verses and the latter with 56, which places both among the top ten contributors. Those ten are as follows:

Shinkei*	123
Sōzei*	114

12. See Okuda Isao, "Renga sakuhin nenpyō kō," *Tōkyō Daigaku Kyōyō Gakubu jinbun kagaku kiyō* 32 (1963); and "Renga sakuhin nenpyō hoi, sono ichi," *Tōkyō Daigaku Kyōyō Gakubu jinbun kagaku* 39 (1966); as well as Akase Shingo, "Manshu-inzō renga sakuhin mokuroku narabi ni nenpyō," *Kokugo kokubun* (January 1978); and *Hyakuin renga kaishi—Manshu-inzō, Kyōto Daigaku kokugo kokubun shiryō sōsho* 49 (Tokyo, 1984).

Emperor Go-Tsuchimikado	108
Senjun*	108
Masahiro	75
Chiun*	66
Sōgi	59
Crown Prince Katsuhito	56
Kensai	52
Sōi*	46

The poets marked with an asterisk are among the "Seven Sages," whose work Sōgi anthologized in his *Chikurinshō* ("Bamboo Grove Collection").[13] Ōuchi Masahiro (1446–95), the great daimyo of western Honshu, was the strongest single patron of the anthology project. Kensai (1452–1510) was Commissioner of *Renga* at Kitano Shrine and Bakufu Laureate (*sōshō,* an appointment by then conferred concurrently with the former), and he collaborated with Sōgi on the work of compilation. Inclusion among the top ten names was to some extent determined by contributions made to the compilation process itself, but even so, it is clear that the avid *renga* activity of the court was unmatched by any other segment of the *renga* community, save for the noncourtier *renga* masters themselves.

Among Go-Tsuchimikado's verses is the following:

This is my life's lot,
and I cannot raise my voice
in words of complaint.

mi o shireba / koto ni idete mo / kakotarezu

Both the one and the other
make this a world of woe.[14]

to ni mo kaku ni mo / uki wa yo no naka

The *maeku* here was composed as a lover's complaint, but Go-Tsuchimikado's link recasts it as a lament on his position as an emperor who suffers both because he presides over a world in turmoil and because his exalted position constrains him from giving vent in

13. Hoshika Sōichi, ed., *Kōhon chikurinshō* (Tokyo: Iwanami Shoten, 1937).
14. Kaneko Kinjirō and Yokoyama Shigeru, eds., *Shinsen tsukubashū* (poems 3,275–76) (Tokyo: Kadokawa Shoten, 1970), 269.

plain words to the pain it causes him. This double burden is what the emperor means by "both the one and the other." The poem is a moving expression of the misery of a monarch reigning amid chaos.

Sōgi and the Imperial House

The interaction between Sōgi and the imperial house was indirect and effected exclusively through intermediaries. The reason for this was Sōgi's social status. Although legend has it that he was the child of an itinerant entertainer, it seems more likely that he was born in Ōmi Province as the offspring of a military family in the service of the Sasaki house, itself of Ōmi Genji lineage.[15] Such ancestry did not permit direct contact with the palace. Crown Prince Katsuhito did listen in person to Sōgi lecture on *Ise monogatari* ("Tales of Ise"), but that occurred at the Fushiminomiya residence and not the imperial palace, and the crown prince had not yet acceded to the throne. The meeting was in any case exceptional; all others were carried out by means of intermediaries.

Sōgi's first recorded contact with the imperial house is found in the *Tokikunikyōki,* the diary of the courtier Yamashina Tokikuni (1452–1503).[16] An entry for the twenty-fourth day of the eighth month, 1474, says that "thirty *renga* verses by Sōgi" were presented to Go-Tsuchimikado. The next instance is also found in an entry in *Tokikunikyōki* for the next year, on the seventh through eleventh days of the fourth month, where it refers to "*renga* from Sōgi" and to several days spent in copying and collating them by courtiers. A work that required several days to copy must have been of considerable length; Kidō Saizō has theorized it may have been an anthology by Sōgi.[17]

Sōgi's relationship with the court, which was to come to fruition in the compilation of the second imperial *renga* anthology, can be dated from the thirty *renga* verses he presented in 1474. A number of questions remain, however, with regard to the circumstances accompanying that first contact. Sōgi's movements during the period show him returning to Kyoto in the autumn of 1473, after eight years spent by and large in the Kantō. Yamana Sōzen (1404–73),

15. See chapter 1 of Kaneko Kinjirō, *Sōgi no seikatsu to sakuhin* (Tokyo, 1983).
16. Text available in 8 vols. as part of *Shiryō sanshū* (Tokyo: Zoku Gunsho Ruijū Kanseikai).
17. Kidō Saizō, *Rengashi ronkō,* vol. 1 (Tokyo: Meiji Shoin, 1971), 442.

commander of the Western Army during the Ōnin War, had died in the third month of that year, and Hosokawa Katsumoto (1430–73), commander of the Eastern Army, in the fifth month, and the conflict was drawing to a conclusion. In the tenth month Sōgi called on Ichijō Kaneyoshi, who was still in Nara in refuge from the fighting, and he passed on to him five hundred *hiki* in coin. Kaneyoshi had had extensive dealings with Sōgi's teacher Sōzei (d. 1455), collaborating with him on a revision of the rules of *renga* (*shikimoku*) and on *Shingyokushū* ("New Collection of Gems"), a *renga* anthology subsequently lost in the Ōnin War. Sōgi's relationship with Kaneyoshi is thought to date from sometime before Sōzei's death. Sōgi had visited Kaneyoshi in Nara during a brief return to the capital from the Kantō in 1469, and they had composed *renga* together at that time.[18] His relationship with Kaneyoshi was no doubt a major factor in enabling him to present the "thirty *renga* verses by Sōgi" to the court in 1474. Sōgi's return to the capital coincided with the beginning of the gradual recrudescence of court *renga* activity after the long fallow period caused by the Ōnin disturbance, and the return of a gifted poet like Sōgi to the *renga* world of the capital generated considerable interest at the palace.[19] It is unclear, however, exactly what hopes Sōgi entertained at this juncture regarding his possible future with the imperial house.

In the fourth month of the following year, 1475, the "*renga* from Sōgi" were presented as his second offering to the court. The event was of marked importance if it is indeed true that an anthology by Sōgi was involved, as would seem to have been the case in light of the time involved in preparing the work for imperial delectation. The work underwent two collations before presentation, and then the emperor ordered it collated yet a third time—*Tokikunikyōki* records him saying on that occasion, "I am very pleased—see that the text is collated once more." This indicates how seriously the project was viewed and how impressive was the size and quality of the result. Kidō makes no further comments about this project, but there is room for further speculation. Sōgi's receipt of a preface for his ten-volume *Chikurinshō* anthology on the twenty-third day of the fifth month of

18. See chapter 3 of Kaneko, *Sōgi no seikatsu.*
19. See "*Shinsen tsukubashū* kankei nenpyō" in Kaneko, *Shinsen tsukubashū no kenkyū*, 775–892. This chronology provides a general overview but is based only on printed sources and is thus incomplete.

the next year, which he had requested from Kaneyoshi in Nara, raises the possibility that the work presented to the palace was the precursor of the *Chikurinshō* anthology. The work for which Sōgi requested a preface no doubt incorporated later revisions, but the original manuscript could certainly have been completed by the fourth month of 1475. If this theory is correct and the collection presented to Go-Tsuchimikado was indeed an early version of *Chikurinshō,* then it clearly was meant to serve as more than a simple aid for composition practice. Kaneyoshi wrote in his preface that he hoped to live long enough to begin work on a second imperial *renga* anthology, *Shoku tsukubashū* ("Later Tsukuba Collection"), as he called it, and that he planned to use *Chikurinshō* along with other private collections as sources of verses for the work. Sōgi probably thought in those terms as well and presented *Chikurinshō* to the court as preparation for the day when Kaneyoshi would begin work on the larger project. Sōgi could not have known at the time that he himself would eventually direct the compilation of *Shinsen tsukubashū,* and he probably looked forward to Kaneyoshi assuming that role, especially in light of the fact that Kaneyoshi himself had written the *Chikurinshō* preface. Kaneyoshi, with Sōgi's help, returned to Kyoto in 1478, but he died in the fourth month of 1481, at the age of seventy-nine, leaving his *Shoku tsukubashū* project unrealized.

By 1476, the year after the presentation of the "*renga* from Sōgi," Sōgi was fully reestablished in the mainstream of *renga* activity in the capital. In the fourth month of that year, he took up residence in his famous cottage, the Shugyokuan. That cottage was next to Irie Palace, another name for Sanjichionji nunnery, located near the intersection of Nishinotōin and Ōgimachi avenues. The nunnery had close ties to the Fushiminomiya family, and daughters of various shoguns resided there from time to time as well. During Sōgi's lifetime the elder sister of Sanjōnishi Sanetaka was mistress of its East Cottage (Tōan). Irie Palace thus served as a convenient meeting place for Sanetaka and Sōgi, who would become increasingly close as the years progressed.[20]

On the eighteenth of the twelfth month of Bunmei 8 (early 1477), Sōgi presented to the emperor a fragment of *Kokinshū* in the hand of Enga (late fifteenth century) and received a *nyōbō hōsho* (a

20. See chapter 6 of Kaneko, *Sōgi no seikatsu.*

letter from one of the ladies-in-waiting who served as the emperor's secretaries) conveying Go-Tsuchimikado's thanks. By this time Sōgi had been initiated into all the "*Kokinshū* Secret Traditions" (*Kokin denju*) by Tō Tsuneyori (1402–84?), and the gift to the palace may have been meant to make clear Sōgi's position in the Nijō orthodoxy, as both Enga and Tsuneyori had studied with Gyōkō (1391–1455) of the Nijō school of poetry.

Sōgi again visited Kaneyoshi in Nara on the twenty-ninth of the seventh month of 1477 and conveyed to him a request for judgments (*gatten*) on a palace linked-verse contest in seventy rounds (*Kinri nanajū-ban renga-awase*) held on the seventh of the same month. Sōgi had been entrusted with the manuscript through the agency of Sanetaka. It was from this year that Sanetaka began to record in his diary his meetings with Sōgi, which were to become increasingly frequent as the years progressed. Sanetaka studied linked verse as well as classics such as *Kokinshū* and *Genji monogatari* with Sōgi, and in return Sanetaka served in his capacity of Palace Chamberlain as intermediary between Sōgi and the emperor and crown prince. Sanetaka later received the "*Kokinshū* Secret Traditions" from Sōgi, and he was instrumental in the realization of the *Shinsen tsukubashū* project. Their close relationship endured until Sōgi's death.

Apart from Sanetaka, Sōgi had contact with the palace through the regent, Konoe Masaie (1444–1505), whom he saw increasingly frequently as the years progressed. Sōgi's disciple Shōhaku (1443–1527) also provided a natural route to palace circles, as he was the younger brother of the Minister of the Center (*naidaijin*), Nakanoin Michihide, and thus of a rank to take part in palace *renga* sessions.[21]

Sōgi's ties with the imperial house, while always indirect, thus increased in frequency over time. That interaction had a variety of aspects. It involved not only the presentation of the instructive works on *renga* and *uta* touched upon earlier, but also judgment of *renga* compositions by the emperor and crown prince. Occasionally Sōgi cast himself in the opposite role and requested imperial judgments on linked verses of his own. In addition, Sōgi presented to the palace reference works on verse composition, and he answered questions regarding the application of *renga* rules. But his most significant

21. See Watanuki, "Go-Tsuchimikadotei rengadan."

dealings with the palace revolved around the compilation of the second imperial *renga* anthology, *Shinsen tsukubashū.*

Judgments on *renga* verses were sometimes requested simply as a form of competitive entertainment, with prizes for the winning efforts. But the more usual and important reason for such requests had long been to improve poetic skill by soliciting the opinion and advice of an experienced teacher. Good verses were marked with a single line (*kagiten*) and especially fine work received a second line (*chōten*). The judgments were often accompanied by concise critical remarks. In the case of the Go-Tsuchimikado court, requests for judgments were made during the Bunmei era (1469–87) to the *renga* master Sugihara Katamori (1418–85), who later in those years took the Buddhist name Sōi. The other notable *renga* masters among his contemporaries had all left the capital to escape the Ōnin War. Some judgments by him survive, including a palace *renga* made on the twenty-second of the eleventh month of Bunmei 11 (early 1480), *Manshu-in* manuscript, graded under the name Katamori, and a solo *renga* (*dokugin*) by Go-Tsuchimikado from the twenty-second of the sixth month of Bunmei 14 (1482), Kokkai Toshokan manuscript, signed with the name Sōi. Sōi was one of the "Seven Sages" anthologized by Sōgi in *Chikurinshō,* and he gave his support to Sōgi when the latter returned to the capital from the Kantō. After Sōi died, on the twenty-eighth of the eleventh month, Bunmei 17 (early 1486), the court sent its requests for grading to Sōgi instead, and a hundred-verse sequence by Go-Tsuchimikado and Katsuhito with judgments by him survives from the Bunmei era.[22] The *hokku* (first verse) and *wakiku* (second verse) read as follows:

> Bunmei [lacuna], seventh month, Yama-nani ["Mountain-something," the *fushimono* title]

> Swaying but slightly,
> so gentle the autumn wind—
> early pampas grass.
> The Emperor

> nabiku yori / akikaze yowashi / hatsu obana

22. Text available in Yamada Tsūkō, comp., *Rengashūsho,* vol. 25 (Seikadō Bunkō, 1830–44).

Falling onto bush clover—
white dewdrops in the morning.
The Prince

mahagi ni utsuru / kesa no shiratsuyu

At the end of the hundred-verse sequence is the notation, "Thirteen verses of note—judgments by Sōgi," and a verse tally (*kuage*) that reads, "The Emperor: fifty verses, six of note; The Prince: fifty verses, seven of note." Though the date of the sequence is unclear, it was probably composed after the death of Sōi in the eleventh month of 1485 and before the end of the Bunmei era on the twentieth day of the seventh month, 1487. It is the oldest extant sequence judged by Sōgi for the palace, and the only such work to survive from the Bunmei era.

Palace sequences judged by Sōgi after the Bunmei era are as follows:

1490
8.17: Two-poet sequence (*ryōgin*) with the emperor and Sanetaka
9.9: Two-poet sequence with the emperor and Sanetaka
1491
4.8: Palace *renga*
1492
12.3: Palace *renga*
1493
3.12: Crown prince's *tsukeku renga*
1495
8.27: Palace *renga*
9.27: Two-poet sequence with the emperor and Sanetaka
1496
8.7: Three-poet sequence (*sangin*) with the emperor, the crown prince, and Sanetaka
10.10: Palace *renga*
1497
9.19: Palace *renga*
1498
(2.8: Comments on a palace thousand-verse *renga*)
6.17: Palace *renga*
10.9: Palace *kōshin renga*
11.3: Palace *kōshin renga*

1499
3.16: Palace *renga*

All the above are taken from references in *Sanetakakōki* except for the crown prince's *tsukeku renga* of 1493, which is recorded in *Tokikunikyōki.* The two-poet sequence with the emperor and Sanetaka from 1495 and the three-poet sequence with the emperor, the crown prince, and Sanetaka from 1496 are extant.[23] The list shows that for every year after the Bunmei era except 1487–89 and 1494, Sōgi was commanded to judge *renga* for the emperor. Such commissions increased markedly in frequency from 1495, the year of the compilation of *Shinsen tsukubashū.* In a year of particular activity, 1498, Sōgi presented judgments on three separate hundred-verse *renga,* as well as comments on a thousand-verse sequence. This indicates that the passion for *renga* at the palace represented a serious, long-term commitment, not simply a temporary enthusiasm accompanying the anthology project.

Of the judged sequences listed above, the palace *renga* on the seventeenth day of the sixth month, 1498, is of particular interest. Sōgi was asked, via a letter by an imperial secretary, to correct the weaknesses of the work and return it to the palace.[24] He did so, and a number of his remarks, preserved by Sanetaka in his diary, are quite severe:

> [With regard to the verse with the word] *ukina* (compromised name)—it can indeed be associated with *hototogisu* (cuckoo), but such a link is difficult, is it not?
>
> *Fukaki no* (deep field), and *naruki nawa* (clapper rope) have been linked to *koto shigeki* (many things), but this should be reconsidered and deleted.
>
> [With regard to the verse that begins with] *waga utanu / yoso no kinuta* (Another's fulling block / that I do not strike)—if you have "Another's fulling block," then "that I do not strike" is otiose.

23. Also available in Yamada, *Rengashūsho.*
24. *Sanetakakōki* (Tokyo: Zoku Gunsho Ruijū Kanseikai, 1958), vol. 11, 443.

> Linking a verse with *yamashita* (foot of the mountain) to one with *hagi* (bush clover) is crude.[25]

The comments run together in Sanetaka's diary but clearly relate to four separate aspects of the sequence. The second and third passages deal with words that should be avoided; the last suggests that limiting the scene to the foot of the mountain in fact weakens the image of the bush clover. Sōgi's comments condemn misuse of words and praise purity of expression, and they are impressive in their unhesitating use of such strong words as "otiose" (*muryoku*) and "crude" (*kitanashi*).

The commission to judge the palace *renga* of the eighth of the second month, 1498, has been listed in parentheses since it did not involve actual judgments but rather comments on a link from the sequence. The link (quoted below) included the compound *minoshirogoromo* (a plain cloth wrap used instead of a straw cape to keep out the rain), and a letter was sent to Sōgi regarding it. Sōgi responded with an explanation and a postscript, which prompted a second *nyōbō hōsho,* the exchange developing into a debate between Sōgi and the palace, with ideological ramifications.[26]

The first letter quotes the verses in question:

All is fallen to ruin
here in my native village.

koko mo kashiko mo / aruru furusato

  How I wish I had
at least a plain cloth wrap
  to cover myself!

sore o dani / minoshirogoromo / kasaneba ya

The letter then asks if it would not be preferable, given the nature of the emperor's *tsukeku* link, for the preceding verse to read:

Cold and fallen to ruin,
a cottage in the wormwood.

25. Ibid.
26. Ibid., 407-9.

arete samukeki / yomogiu no yado

Sōgi responds by saying that *Gosenshū* (951) number 1,355 is the appropriate poetic source (*honka*) for the *tsukeku*:

Dew must lie deep
on the blades of grass in
the mountain village.
Though it is not finely stitched,
take this cloth wrap as a rain cape!

yamazato no / kusaba no tsuyu wa / shigekaramu /
minoshirogoromo / nuwazu to mo kiyo

The *maeku,* he goes on, should in this case include the words *ame* (rain) or *tsuyu* (dew), but it is also acceptable as it is since both are implied by *furusato* (native village) in the context of another verse that includes the phrase *ame tsuyu mo / tamaranu furusato* (My native village/ unsheltered from the rain and dew).

The second letter takes issue with Sōgi's interpretations of the original link and insists that it was based instead on a prose source (*honzetsu*) from the "Hatsune" ("The First Warbler") chapter of *Genji monogatari,* where *minoshirogoromo* is used in a conversation between Genji and Suetsumuhana. The letter theorizes that the emperor employed the word in association with *furusato* in the previous verse because Genji in that scene used the same word in a poem:

Having come to call
and view the spring branches in
my native village,
I see a blossom unlike
any other in the world![27]

furusato no / haru no kozue ni / tazunekite /
yo no tsune naranu / hana o miru kana

The alternative *maeku* suggested in the letter emphasizes the connection to Suetsumuhana through the phrase *yomogiu no yado* (cottage in the wormwood), a reference to Suetsumuhana's residence and the "Yomogiu" ("The Wormwood Patch") chapter of *Genji*

27. Genji puns on *hana,* referring both to blossoms and to Suetsumuhana's conspicuous nose.

monogatari, in which the lady figures. The letter wonders if Sōgi had overlooked this connection.

The original exchange was in greater detail than that presented here, but the nature of the difference of opinion should be clear. The *nyōbō hōsho* simply emphasizes the scene in *Genji monogatari,* without inquiring into the emotions of the poet. Sōgi, by contrast, sees the pathos in having only a poor cloth wrap instead of a straw rain cape, and he emphasizes this in his interpretation of the link with the preceding verse. The emperor displays intellectual interest in classical quotations; Sōgi, a response to the pathos of life.

Besides judging palace *renga,* Sōgi also wrote reference works on the art of composition and on *renga* rules. The two works mentioned earlier, "thirty *renga* verses by Sōgi" (1474) and "*renga* from Sōgi" (1475), were both useful for reference, and he thereafter presented the additional matter listed below:

1486

9.17: Sōgi presents to the palace a copy of *Dōmei meisho* ("Famous Places with the Same Names")[28] by Ton'a (1289–1372), copied by Gyōkō.

1488

Intercalary 11: Sōgi presents a lecture series on *Ise monogatari* at the residence of Prince Fushiminomiya Kunitaka. On the twelfth of the same month the crown prince attends.

1489

11.16: Sōgi brings from Yamaguchi a copy of *Jūmon saihishō* ("Most Secret Treatise on Ten Inquiries")[29] by Nijō Yoshimoto (1320–88) and gives it to Sanetaka to present to the palace.

1490

9.24: Sanetaka reads a treatise on linked verse (*renga shōmono*) by Sōgi to the emperor.

1493

The matter of small revisions in *Renga shinshiki* ("The New Rules of Linked Verse")[30] is conveyed from the emperor to Sōgi by Konoe Masaie (source: *Go-Hōkō'in ki*).

28. A reference to the fourth section of the poet's *Seiashō* ("Notes from a Frog in a Well"), available in Sasaki Nobutsuna, comp., *Nihon kagaku taikei,* vol. 5 (Tokyo: Kazama Shobō, 1957).
29. Text available in Ijichi Tetsuo and Kidō Saizō, eds., *Rengaronshū haironshū,* vol. 66 of *Nihon koten bungaku taikei* (Tokyo: Iwanami Shoten, 1961).
30. Text available in Hoshika Sōichi and Yamada Yoshio, *Renga hōshiki kōyō* (Tokyo: Iwanami Shoten, 1936).

1496

9.21: Sōgi presents *Sōgi gojūnikajō no kiraimono* ("Fifty-two Articles on *kiraimono* by Sōgi")[31] to the throne after an inquiry on *kiraimono* (rules on proscribed repetitions in renga sequences) from *nyōbō hōsho* on the nineteenth of the same month.

1497

9.12: Sanetaka peruses a treatise on linked verse (*renga shōmono*) by Sōgi at the palace.

The nature of the treatises on linked verse mentioned in the entries for 1490 and 1497 is unclear—they may or may not be identical. To judge from the term *shōmono,* they were most likely collections of linked verse with commentary added. Sōgi wrote a number of such works, including *Chikurinshō no chū* ("Comments on *Chikurinshō*"), *Yuki no keburi* ("Misty Snow"), *Guku wakuraba* ("My 'Withered Leaves'"), and *Shitakusa chū* ("Comments on 'Undergrowth'"). He also prepared commentaries on smaller verse collections, as well as works on *renga* theory that centered on commentary, such as *Oi no susami* ("An Old Man's Diversions") and *Sōgi hokku hanshi* ("Judgments on Sōgi's *Hokku*").[32] It is possible that the *renga shōmono* in question refer to one or two of his commentaries on collections of linked verse, but there is no way to be sure at this time.

Sōgi's contribution to the court in the area of *renga* rules included the above-mentioned *Sōgi gojūnikajō no kiraimono,* written in 1495 in response to questions on the subject.[33] Already in 1493, the palace had broached the question of revising the standard set of linked-verse rules, *Renga shinshiki,* and Sōgi's opinion had been solicited. After the death of Go-Tsuchimikado, a revision and en-

31. *Sōgi gojūnikajō no kiraimono.* No printed text of this work is available, but for a remarks on it see Morozumi, "Go-Tsuchimikadotei rengadan."

32. Printed texts as follows: for *Chikurinshō no chū* and *Yuki no keburi,* see Yokoyama Shigeru, ed., *Chikurinshō kochū* (Tokyo: Kadokawa Shoten, 1969); for *Guku wakuraba* and *Shitakusa chū,* see Kaneko Kinjirō, ed., *Renga kochūshaku shū* (Tokyo: Kadokawa Shoten, 1979); for *Oi no susami* and *Sōgi hokku hanshi,* see Kidō Saizō, ed., *Rengaronshū 2,* in *Chūsei no bungaku* (Tokyo: Miyai Shoten, 1981).

33. On the court debate surrounding the rule revisions see Shimazu Tadao, "Kensai zōdan oboegaki," in Kaneko Kinjirō, ed., *Renga kichō bunken shūsei kinen ronshū, Renga kenkyū no tenkai* (Tokyo: Benseisha, 1985), 98.

largement was completed by Shōhaku in the sixth month of 1501 and given the name *Renga shinshiki tsuika narabi ni shinshiki kon'an tō* ("The New Rules of Linked Verse, with New Ideas on the New Rules and Additional Comments").[34] Nine articles overlap in content with the fifty-two Sōgi presented in 1495.[35] It is as yet unknown, however, why only nine of Sōgi's fifty-two sections were included in Shōhaku's version. Sōgi added comprehensive remarks on *kiraimono* at the end of his work, giving valuable glimpses into his general attitude. One sentence reads, "If His Majesty observes the *kiraimono* in every case, he may often find it difficult to compose," which indicates that Sōgi did not view the rules as ironclad.

At the end of his remarks, however, Sōgi states, "Though it is not always possible, one hopes that the principle of avoiding *rinne* will be closely observed." For Sōgi, the avoidance of *rinne* (repetition of an element appearing in a previous verse) was the essential purpose of the body of *renga* rules. All *renga* sequences develop according to two basic concepts, linking (*tsukeai*) and variation (*yukiyō*), and the *renga* rules, called either *shikimoku* or *kiraimono*, ensure continual variation by avoiding *rinne*. The enormous breadth and minute detail of the *renga* rules are all devoted to the basic purposes of ensuring variation and determining the character of the successive verses of a sequence. Sōgi insisted that *rinne* was inimical to the shifts in lexical and thematic categories that constitute the essence of the beauty of linked verse, and he directed the emperor's attention to this central pitfall in *renga* composition. The avoidance of *rinne* and the focus on pathos, seen earlier in his comments on the link involving the word *minoshirogoromo*, are basic concepts in the poetic philosophy that Sōgi propounded in his writings for the imperial house.

The Imperial House and *Shinsen tsukubashū*

Sōgi's closest interaction with the imperial house occurred during the compilation of *Shinsen tsukubashū*. It will be recalled that Ichijō Kaneyoshi had earlier planned an imperially sponsored sequel to *Tsukubashū* to be titled *Shoku tsukubashū* and that *Chikurinshō* was to have provided valuable raw material for the purpose, as

34. See n. 30 above.
35. See Morozumi, "Go-Tsuchimikadotei rengadan."

indicated in Kaneyoshi's preface to that work. Kaneyoshi's death in 1481 cut short the proposal, and in the end it was Sōgi himself who took responsibility for compiling a sequel, under the titular direction of Kaneyoshi's son Fuyuyoshi (1464–1514). It is not clear exactly when this arrangement was finalized, but the events leading to it can be traced with some certainty.

One early development worthy of note was Sōgi's visit to the daimyo Ōuchi Masahiro, head of the influential Ōuchi house in western Honshu. Sōgi recounted the trip in his *Tsukushi no michi no ki* ("Account of a Kyushu Journey") of 1480.[36] His main purpose at that time seems to have been to secure backing for a new *waka* anthology.[37] Thereafter Sōgi was appointed Commissioner of *Renga* at Kitano Shrine and Laureate on the twenty-eighth of the third month, 1488, by Shogun Ashikaga Yoshihisa (1465–89), following the death of Sōi, the previous holder of those offices. The proposed *Shoku tsukubashū* project was no doubt one of Sōgi's concerns at that time, but his energies were primarily directed toward providing cooperation for the imperial *waka* anthology project then receiving the active support of Yoshihisa.

But on the twenty-seventh of the third month of 1489, the year after Sōgi's appointment as laureate, the shogun suddenly died at the age of twenty-four while encamped at Magari in Ōmi Province. The hope that he had inspired among both his supporters and the poetic establishment was shattered by his death. The enormity of the loss can be seen by the fact that Sōgi again set out for Ōuchi Masahiro's capital at Yamaguchi only two days after Yoshihisa's demise. He returned to Kyoto on the seventeenth of the ninth month of that year, and for a time he worked to resuscitate the *waka* anthology project, only to see it abandoned soon thereafter.[38] On the third day of the twelfth month Sōgi resigned his positions as Commissioner of *Renga* at Kitano Shrine and Laureate. This was natural in the aftermath of the death of the shogun who had appointed him, but it probably also reflected a loss of faith in the bakufu itself, an institution all the more

36. Text available in Kaneko Kinjirō, *Sōgi tabi no ki shichū* (Tokyo: Ōfūsha, 1975).
37. See chapter 7 of Kaneko, *Sōgi no seikatsu*.
38. For more information on Sōgi and the plan to compile a new imperial *waka* anthology, see Kaneko, *Shinsen tsukubashū no kenkyū*, 332–47.

enfeebled by Yoshihisa's loss. It was also at this point that Sōgi probably ceased to hope that the bakufu would underwrite a new *renga* anthology, and he began to look instead to the great political power and literary commitment of the Ōuchi daimyo and to the growing enthusiasm for linked verse within the imperial house. Sōgi's decision to approach those two quarters to obtain support for an anthology project under his own management probably coalesced after his resignation from his bakufu appointments.

The month after Sōgi stepped down, the retired shogun Yoshimasa died, further weakening the military government. Thereafter, in the ninth month of 1490, Sōgi composed a solo votive hundred-verse sequence for Sumiyoshi, another shrine connected with poetry. The *hokku*:

> May Sumiyoshi's pines
> serve as a landmark for those
> traveling on the way.[39]
>
> suminoe no / matsu koso michi o / shirube nare

The preface relates that the sequence was a *musō no renga*, the *hokku* having come to Sōgi in a dream (*musō*) in the winter of the previous year. It would seem to be more than simple coincidence that Sōgi resigned his bakufu posts at the same time, on the third of the twelfth month. In fact, the sequence most likely symbolized a conscious move away from the bakufu-affiliated Kitano Shrine and toward a new spiritual commitment to the gods of Sumiyoshi. Though the main Sumiyoshi Shrine was located in Settsu Province, it can be supposed that Sōgi was also thinking of the Sumiyoshi Shrine on the Ōuchi lands to the west. But the fact that more than nine months passed between the dream itself and the completion of the votive sequence suggests that doubts had to be overcome before Sōgi could fully commit himself to his change of allegiance. According to *Kitano shake nikki,* the annals of Kitano Shrine, his successor to the two bakufu-appointed posts, Kensai, had in the fifth month of the same year traveled to Kyushu and called on Ōuchi Masahiro. He had returned to Kyoto in the sixth month of the next year, 1491, and it is

39. The text of this sequence is available in Ijichi Tetsuo and Kaneko Kinjirō, eds., *Sōgi kushū* (Tokyo: Kadokawa Shoten, 1979), 389–92.

thought to have been at about this time that Masahiro committed himself to underwriting the compilation of a new *renga* anthology. His decision came at a time when the entire *renga* establishment was displaying new energy, spurred by the emperor and his court who, as pointed out earlier, had been composing *renga* with growing frequency since 1480.

Shinsen tsukubashū itself was completed in 1495, and the court made a major contribution to the project. A deadline for the submission of verses had been set for the fourteenth of the fifth month of that year, and the palace had sent material without delay to Sōgi's Shugyokuan residence via Sanetaka.[40] The following entries for *Sanetakakōki* record the nature of the deliveries:

2.20: *Renga* from previous years (ca. 1478–94)
2.29: *Wakan renku* sequences from previous years (one box)
3.3: Compositions by Retired Emperor Go-Hanazono and others
3.19: Solo sequence by the same retired emperor
3.27: Thousand-verse sequences from previous years (one box)
5.16: *Renga* sessions from the time of Retired Emperor Go-Komatsu

The very large amount of material provided by the court in the second and third months was further augmented by the verses of Emperor Go-Komatsu (1377–1433; r. 1382–1412) in the fifth, in response to a last-minute expansion in the scope of the project. The palace was also the source of a solo thousand-verse sequence and a collection of loose pages by the *renga* master Ninzei (fl. 1440–55), sent on the twenty-third of the first month, and of a box of verses by the late shogun Yoshimasa and his consort, Hino Tomiko (1440–96), delivered on the day of the deadline. The fact that the last was sent via the court suggests the depths to which bakufu influence had fallen and, by contrast, the importance the palace had assumed in the anthology project.

Work at Sōgi's residence proceeded quickly. Already by the fifth of the sixth month the rough manuscript was finished, and on the

40. The information in Ijichi and Kaneko, *Sōgi kushū*, on the course of the compilation process has been summarized in Kaneko, *Shinsen tsukubashū no kenkyū*, 332–47.

twenty-first a preliminary copy (*nakagaki-bon*) had been sent to the palace for imperial evaluation. Just at that point, however, the emperor fell ill, and the copy had to be returned, forcing a delay.

The compilers faced other trials and disappointments during the course of the work in the form of adverse criticism of the project from disaffected quarters. An entry for the fifth of the third month in *Daijō-in jisha zōjiki* ("Affairs of the Temples and Shrines of the Daijō-in") reads, "I have heard rumors that the *Shinsen tsukubashū* project cannot be completed."[41] One problem involved a famous conflict between Sōgi and Kensai over the question of *hokku* by Dōkū (Hosokawa Shigeyuki; 1434–1511). As Kensai was the current holder of the bakufu *renga* posts, it was natural for him to support Dōkū, who was a major force in the bakufu government. But the argument was finally settled in accordance with Sōgi's original wishes. Another was criticism by Anegakōji Mototsuna (d. 1504), a courtier and *renga* enthusiast who cooperated in the project. After the preliminary manuscript of the anthology had been returned unpresented due to the emperor's illness, Sanetaka recorded in his diary Mototsuna's remark that "the apportionment of verses in the anthology seems extremely unfair." In the course of his work on the project, Mototsuna had been privy to a number of very specific complaints from other courtiers. Sanetaka himself had come under attack, and his remark in his diary in self-defense, "I had nothing to do with the decision," suggests that some of the ill feeling was directed at the large number of his verses chosen for the collection. Sanetaka also records in an entry for the second of the seventh month that Sōgi had come to see him, complaining of accusations made by Kensai via Prince Tadatomi, head of the Department of Shinto Affairs. The next day Sanetaka sent a letter on the matter to Crown Prince Katsuhito and received a letter in the prince's own hand in return, settling the affair. Clearly, then, the dissatisfaction and criticism attending the anthology project reached the ears of the emperor and crown prince, but the preliminary copy was nevertheless completed without a major rupture thanks to their strong support.

After the return of the preliminary copy due to the emperor's illness, the project lost momentum, and it was dealt a further blow

41. *Daijō-in jisha zōjiki*. 12 vols. In *Zoku shiryō taisei* (Tokyo: Rinsen Shoten, 1978).

when fire broke out in the residence of Anegakōji Mototsuna, who had been ordered to make the final fair copy. Both the manuscript and the paper for the final copy were lost in the blaze. During this same period Sōgi traveled twice to Ikeda in Settsu Province, where Shōhaku lived, to recover from his exertions on the project and the strain from the criticism it was then receiving. Perhaps to encourage him, the palace on the twentieth of the eighth month asked him to judge an imperial *renga* sequence. The request was accompanied by a *nyōbō hōsho,* saying that although Sōgi was in retirement in the country, the emperor had for some time been looking forward to requesting his judgments. The document also asked him to present separate pages with general comments on the verses. Sōgi's response is preserved in *Sanetakakōki*:

> I humbly return the linked-verse sequence. With regard to the verses therein, I think the word *yūzuki* (evening moon) is undesirable. Furthermore, *nagaki yo no koro* (time of long nights) would be better changed to *yo no nagaki koro* (time when nights are long). And instead of *chikaki mo e tote / negae kano kuni* (The other shore near, one thinks/ to pray for the Promised Land), one might say *chikaki e ni to* . . . (The other shore near, I think . . .). Since I was directed to make these remarks, I have taken the liberty to do so. Please do me the honor of conveying them to the throne.
>
> With deep reverence,
> Sōgi
>
> Eighth month, twentieth day
> To Lord Nakazawa

Sōgi's reply to the *nyōbō hōsho* from the palace was doubly indirect, being addressed not to Sanetaka but to his secretary, Lord Nakazawa. The first of Sōgi's opinions, criticizing the word *yūzuki,* is reflected in other contemporary works on *renga* composition such as *Ginkishō* and *Usuhanazakura* ("Pale Cherry Blossoms"), the latter written for Dōkū by Kensai in 1492.[42] The emendation of *nagaki yo no koro* was to achieve smoother flow. The choice of *chikaki e ni to,* which would seem to imply a first-person subject, instead of *chikaki*

42. *Usuhanazakura* is available in vol. 17 (no. 496) of *Zoku gunsho ruijū*; the manuscript of *Ginkishō* may be found in vol. 1 of *Renga gasshū* (Tokyo: Teikoku Toshokan).

mo e tote was probably because it forms a more natural connection with *negae kano kuni*. The word *e* seems to be used as a pivot word (*kakekotoba*) to mean both *en* (bond or opportunity) and *e* (inlet), here meaning the "other shore" (*higan*), that is, *pāramitā*, Buddhist nirvana. Sōgi's remarks demonstrate a deep sensitivity to minute variations in diction, and it was probably something of a relief for him to immerse himself in such matters after the months of political struggle surrounding the compilation of the anthology.

The fair copy of *Shinsen tsukubashū* was finally completed on the first day of the ninth month of 1495, and on the twenty-sixth Sanetaka presented it to the throne, this time with no hindrances. The emperor conveyed his approbation to Sōgi via a *nyōbō hōsho*. Moreover, the document conferring on the work the status of imperially recognized anthology (*junchokusenshū*) was backdated to the twentieth of the sixth month, the day before the original presentation of the preliminary copy. This was not the only example of such backdating, but it must have been gratifying to those concerned, after the added months of criticism suffered when the presentation was postponed due to the emperor's illness.

The anthology finished, Sōgi went again to Settsu Province, returning to Kyoto on the ninth of the eleventh month. During his trip he probably announced the completion of the project to the gods of Sumiyoshi Shrine. It would have been natural for him to do so, since his retreat in Settsu is thought to have been located between Sumiyoshi Shrine and the city of Sakai.[43] Five years had passed since he resolved to embark on *Shinsen tsukubashū* and completed the Sumiyoshi *musō* solo sequence in the ninth month of 1490.

The day after returning to the capital, Sōgi presented judgments requested earlier on a two-poet linked verse by the emperor and Sanetaka. He singled out nine verses by each for praise and chose one of the emperor's verses as the best of all. The first three verses[44]:

How deeply green
they tint the pine trees—
chilling showers!
The Emperor

midori koku / matsu o ba somuru / shigure kana

43. Kaneko, *Sōgi no seikatsu*, 78.
44. Yamada, *Rengashūsho*.

The many colors of the ivy
are enriched by the dew.
Sanetaka

iromeku tsuta no / tsuyu no hitoshio

At the end of the road
over which the moon descends,
night starts to lighten.
The Emperor

tsuki no yuku / yamaji no sue ni / yo wa akete

The sequence was composed on the twenty-seventh of the ninth month, the day after the presentation of *Shinsen tsukubashū* to the emperor. His *hokku* therefore should be construed as a congratulatory piece, with the pines, symbolizing the way of linked verse, taking on a richer green because of the cold rains, here indicating the anthology. It seems likely that Sōgi was asked to judge the work in order that he might enjoy this oblique praise from the emperor.

On the same day that Sōgi returned his judgments on the two-poet *renga*, he also presented two *hokku* he had composed that winter while in Settsu. They are recorded in *Sanetakakōki*:

Hokku composed by Sōgi while in Settsu:

Days and months have passed,
and now even the sun and moon
grow damp in cold rains.[45]

meguri kite / kage mo shigururu / tsukihi kana

Could this refer to the time since last spring? How very moving.

Wait before you fall!
More cold rains have yet to tint
the faintly colored leaves.[46]

machite chire / mata ya shigure no / usumomiji

45. *Uraba* no. 340, in Ijichi and Kaneko, *Sōgi kushū*.
46. *Uraba* no. 355, in Ijichi and Kaneko, *Sōgi kushū*.

Both verses are also found in Sōgi's last collection of verses, *Uraba* ("Late Leaves"), the former preceded by the comment, "On feelings in early winter," and the latter, "At the residence of Irie Sakyōnosuke." The former verse is difficult to interpret—Sōgi's prefatory comment suggests it was made on the emotions of the moment, while Sanetaka's remark says it may refer to all the intervening months since the previous spring. The verse was composed in response to the *hokku* the emperor made for his session with Sanetaka on the twenty-seventh of the ninth month, and it likewise refers to cold rains. But Sōgi's poem is a lament, and he uses the rains to suggest instead the pain caused him by prolonged criticism during the *Shinsen tsukubashū* project. His verse implies that the memory of his struggle makes even the light of the sun and the moon (Sōgi uses *tsukihi* to mean both "sun and moon" and "days and months") seem dampened by the cold rains. Commentators have suggested, too, that the light of both sun and moon is also an indirect reference to the beneficence of the emperor. Be that as it may, the emperor's *hokku* from the session with Sanetaka and Sōgi's *hokku* in response are both bound up with the *Shinsen tsukubashū* anthology project, and they memorialize the union it occasioned between the poetic zeal of Go-Tsuchimikado and Katsuhito and the deep dedication of Sōgi to the way of linked verse.

But these were by no means the last of the events accompanying the completion of *Shinsen tsukubashū*. On the thirteenth of the twelfth month Sōgi was presented with three of the "six famous types of incense" (*rokushu meikō*): "evening plum blossoms" (*yūbaika*), "chamberlain" (*jijū*), and "lotus leaves" (*kayō*). "Chamberlain" figures in *Genji monogatari* and was undoubtedly deeply appreciated by Sōgi, who was well versed in the way of incense (*kōdō*). On the fifteenth, he sampled the incense at Sanetaka's mansion, where the two men congratulated themselves on the successful completion of the enterprise.

On the same day, the fifteenth, topics were distributed for a hundred-poem votive *uta* offering Sōgi had initiated for Sumiyoshi Shrine in the Ōuchi province of Nagato. Poems were collected from thirty poets in Kyoto who had been involved in work on *Shinsen tsukubashū*, including the emperor, Crown Prince Katsuhito, various nobles, and *renga* masters from outside the court. On the twenty-seventh of the intercalary second month of the following year, 1496,

Sanetaka wrote the postscript for the assembled compositions. The effort demonstrates the extent to which all acknowledged the debt owed the Ōuchi house for its support of the *Shinsen tsukubashū* project.

It was also on the twenty-seventh of the intercalary second month that Sanetaka wrote a postscript to *Sōgi kushū,* a collection of one hundred *tsukeku* and fifty *hokku* by the *renga* master. These were verses for which Sōgi had requested the judgments of Go-Tsuchimikado. The emperor had initially demurred but had in the end been prevailed upon by Sanetaka to accept. Entries in *Sanetakakōki* tell of the pains the emperor took with the work. *Sōgi kushū* no longer exists, but Sanetaka preserved his postscript in his diary:

> Postscript to a Scroll of Imperial Judgments
>
> Since imperial judgments were requested for these verses by the priest Sōgi, I several times brought the matter to the attention of the throne, and the judgments by the imperial brush were bestowed. Surely this is a source of happiness in Sōgi's old age and a proud moment for the way of poetry. It is a cause for deepest gratitude. Fifth year of Meiō [1496], intercalary second month.
>
> Akai Shūi [cipher (*kao*)]

Sanetaka at the time was a Provisional Major Counsellor (*gondainagon*) and Chamberlain (*jijū*) and so signed himself by the alternate names for those offices. The imperial judgments were another reward for Sōgi's recent efforts, and though it is not expressly stated, the reason Sanetaka found it necessary to broach the matter several times was probably because of the emperor's reluctance to remark on the verses of his own poetic advisor.

Conclusion

The foregoing has examined the relationship between the imperial house and Sōgi, paying particular attention to the compilation of *Shinsen tsukubashū*. Throughout that process, sovereign and *renga* master enjoyed a relationship of close cooperation, and the criticism the project received before compilation served only to strengthen the bonds uniting them.

For Sōgi, the imperial house would always be a distant world, reachable only indirectly due to his humble birth. He saw it both as a lofty guarantor of the *Shinsen tsukubashū* anthology and as a center of unsurpassed potential for the further propagation of the way of linked verse. The direction Sōgi provided the sovereign and court, based primarily on empirical analysis of actual verses rather than on general theoretical observations, was aimed at the preservation of the poetic orthodoxy and at the same time reflected great hope for the increasing prosperity of linked verse in the future. The personal bonds engendered during Sōgi's years as imperial tutor became his single greatest source of spiritual support during his work on *Shinsen tsukubashū*. No more vivid example exists of a relationship of trust based on and fostered through the composition of linked verse. The throne, for its part, appreciated Sōgi for efforts he made to improve its financial condition, but it always valued him primarily for his poetic genius. It was Sōgi who provided the sure direction for the palace's bourgeoning *renga* enthusiasm and who finally supervised its coalescence into an eternal monument, *Shinsen tsukubashū*. In return, the imperial house gave him numerous indications of gratitude and undivided faith. In the aftermath of the devastation of the Ōnin War, this mutual faith, born of shared commitment to literature, greatly contributed to the further development of the linked-verse art.

Sanjōnishi Sanetaka, Takeno Jōō, and an Early Form of *Iemoto Seido*

Kumakura Isao
Translated by Steven D. Carter

In the context of Japanese literary history, it was the world of linked verse (*renga*) that first produced professional artists. As Shimazu Tadao has shown, the word *rengashi,* "master of linked verse," already appears here and there in records beginning early in the fifteenth century, when a professional consciousness began to emerge among commoners who enjoyed composing linked verse.[1]

An example reflecting this historical development can be found in the entry for the twenty-first day of the third month of 1408 in *Noritokikyōki,* a diary kept by a court noble of the time.[2] There it is recorded that one lay monk, Hatano Genki, identified as a "master of linked verse," received 5,000 *hiki* as a gratuity for his work as scribe at a linked-verse meeting. Thus, by that era masters of linked verse, even if they held other occupations concurrently, were receiving considerable sums from their poetic activities. This trend continued, until, by the late Muromachi period, masters of linked verse such as Sōgi (1421–1502), Sōchō (1448–1532), Bontanka Shōhaku (1443–1527), and Satomura Jōha (1524–1602) appear to have provided complete support for themselves via income received in their activities as linked-verse poets. From this we can also assume the advent, in the

1. See Shimazu Tadao, *Renga no kenkyū* (Tokyo: Kadokawa Shoten, 1973), 267–325.
2. The noble was Yamashina Noritoki (1337–1410). The text is available in *Shiryō sanshū* (Tokyo: Zoku Gunsho Ruijū Kanseikai).

historical background, of patrons who supported these masters of the art.

The world of linked verse was made up of various kinds of people, which can be categorized in this way:

(1) Nobles (*kuge*) who possessed traditional knowledge of and association with the poetic traditions of the imperial court. As in the case of Sanjōnishi Sanetaka (1455–1537), such nobles attended linked-verse meetings and influenced the art greatly as men of authority in the poetic world, but they cannot be called masters of linked verse themselves.

(2) *Rengashi* who were recognized as specialists in the professional sense. This category would include Sōgi, Sōchō, Jōha, and others alluded to above.

(3) Those who were known as *rengashi* but had other occupations or status as warriors or townsmen. One of these would be the Sakai townsman Takeno Jōō (1502–55), about whom more shall be offered below.

(4) Those who composed linked verse but were not referred to as *rengashi.* These people were not truly masters of linked verse, and they thus had other occupations and did not accept disciples in the art. In a word, they were amateurs, and they existed in great numbers.

(5) Warrior chieftains who supported *rengashi,* as they did other *dōbōshū* (coteries of artists retained as arbiters of taste, teachers, and curators), asking them, for example, to compose dedicatory sequences as prayers for victory in battle. Although such men did of course participate in the composition of linked verse, how much they actually knew about the art is unknown. In other words, they were simply "receptors" (*kyōjusha*), who also acted as patrons in political and economic terms.

How these various men interacted with each other, and in what ways those interactions had to do with the nature of linked verse itself, is what will be discussed in this paper.

The men who belonged to categories one and two above were not blessed with the most fortunate economic circumstances. One example is Sanjōnishi Sanetaka, a man of ancient pedigree but shrunken fortunes whose family suffered greatly from the degradations of the Ōnin War of 1467–77. During the fighting, which took place in the streets of the city, the Sanjōnishi home was razed, sending Sanetaka and his family to a temple on the northern outskirts of the city for some years where they lived a straitened existence. Even after his return in the fall of 1473, Sanetaka was in difficult circumstances financially much of the time—all of this despite his status as the heir of a noble clan, which eventually (in 1506) won him appointment as Palace Minister of Senior Second rank.

However, Sanetaka was able to make a living for himself and his family through various means, including his work as a literatus with a fine reputation deriving from his own talents and his years of study under masters, including the scion of the Asukai family, who inducted him into the secret teachings of classical *uta*, and the *rengashi* Sōgi, who acted as his teacher in the art of linked verse. In his time, such knowledge was in demand, in particular from men of the warrior class who were anxious to identify themselves with the old traditions, but also from wealthy townsmen and higher-ranking aristocrats. Sanetaka made his living, to a large extent, by answering those needs.

But just how much income did a man like Sanetaka realize from his work in linked verse? Surely not as much as the 5,000 *hiki* received by the lay monk Genki in the incident recounted above, which was a very considerable sum indeed. A more typical example is one noted in Sanetaka's diary for the year 1524, when he was invited to a linked-verse meeting held by a certain Tanemura Sadakazu and received a gratuity of 1,500 *hiki* plus an allowance for food and drink, a gift that pleased him as "a most extravagant sum." Since prices at the time were figured at approximately one *hiki* (ten *mon*) to one *shō*, 1,500 *hiki* would be the equivalent of fifteen measures (*koku*) of rice. If we take Sanetaka's surprise over his "most extravagant sum" at face value, however, even this example may not be an accurate index of actual practice at the time. Gratuities for participation in linked-verse meetings probably amounted to less than this in most cases, perhaps to between three and five hundred *hiki* as a general rule.

Thus, even if some of the highest ranking members of the nobility were able to reward poets for their services—as for instance, Konoe Hisamichi (d. 1544), who invited Bontanka Shōhaku to lecture on *Genji monogatari,* offering a gratuity in payment—such extravagance was not possible for middling nobles like Sanetaka. On the contrary, Sanetaka was often in the position of being paid for his participation in literary functions, as in the case of the linked-verse meeting held by Tanemura Sadakazu mentioned above, to which Sanetaka was invited via the introduction of the *rengashi* Sōchō, himself, of course, also receiving a gratuity from the warlord as well. In this sense it may be said that those in categories one and two both required patrons for their support.

Thanks to the evidence provided by his large diary,[3] Sanetaka's financial situation is well known. According to Haga Koshirō, Sanetaka's annual income, if all sources paid faithfully and consistently, would have totaled approximately 26,350 *hiki*—a figure amounting to more than 263 measures of rice. It was derived from levies on his estates and from guilds. In the late Muromachi period, however, private estate revenues were constantly encroached upon by local landlords, and guild rights—judged by traders to be parasitic—were also subject to intimidation. The relatively weak Sanjōnishi family could therefore not be assured of such an income year by year. This meant that Sanetaka in many cases suffered frequent reductions in income. The following is a breakdown of his income for the year 1526[4]: income from estate rights, 27 percent; income from guilds, 41 percent; income from special sources, 27 percent; and income from loans, 5 percent. The 27 percent referred to as "income from special sources" of course corresponds to Sanetaka's earnings from his work as a traditional poet and attendance at poetry gatherings, including linked-verse meetings. Without that income it is doubtful that the account books of the Sanjōnishi house could have remained in balance.

Of course, this does not mean that literary work was the only, or even the major, source of Sanetaka's support. In fact, for Sanetaka, it was the great generals of the warrior class who acted as primary financial patrons, with Hatakeyama Yoshifusa, *shugo* of Noto, contributing 10,000 *hiki* toward the construction of a new family home and also sending substantial cash gifts from time to time. But it was the disciples he gained through his work as a poet and scholar that were there offering support against the immediate demands of everyday life.

One such disciple was Takeno Jōō, a wealthy townsmen from the port city of Sakai, a thriving commercial center located on the coast of Osaka Bay. Judging from records that refer to him as *kawaya*

3. Sanjōnishi Kin'osa and Takahashi Ryūzō, eds., *Sanetakakōki*, 15 vols. (Tokyo: Zoku Gunsho Ruijū Kanseikai, 1955–67).

4. Haga Kōshirō, *Sanjōnishi Sanetaka* (Tokyo: Yoshikawa Kobunkan, 1960), 205.

("leather dealer"), Jōō may have come from a family of warehousemen who traded in leather and hides. Whatever the case, he went on to become one of the earliest and greatest of late Muromachi tea masters (he was the teacher of Sen Rikyū [1522–91], whose ideal of *wabicha*, or "poverty tea," was inherited largely from Jōō).[5]

However, a contemporary record notes that tea was not always Jōō's occupation, for "until the age of thirty," it says, "he was a master of linked verse."[6] Further, he also studied traditional *uta* poetry, in which he was tutored by Sanetaka, receiving a copy of the famous *Eiga taigai* ("An Outline for Composing *Uta*," 1221?) as part of his course. It was Jōō's study of the high artistic ideals of that poetic text, in fact, that supposedly led him to become a master of the relatively new art of tea.

Jōō's relationship with Sanetaka began in the latter's last years. During the third month of 1528, when Sanetaka was seventy-four and Jōō twenty-seven, the noble's diary records that when Jōō came to visit he brought gifts of sake and fish and 200 *hiki* in cash. Later, in the sixth month of the same year, when Sanetaka was beginning a series of lectures on *Ise monogatari*, Jōō offered his teacher more food and 500 *hiki* that he brought again at the end of the month. And if we look at Sanetaka's diary for the next year, we find similar exchanges here and there, with a large sum of 1,000 *hiki* coming at the end of the year, which delights Sanetaka as an "unexpected" event.

What made Sanetaka even more happy, however, was Jōō's arrangement at the same time, by some unknown means, to secure payment of the *nengu*, or yearly revenue due for land rent, from one of the Sanjōnishi family's uncooperative estate managers. The estate involved was Misunoshō in Yamashiro, the proprietary rights to which the Sanjōnishi family had held for many years. Although the actual amount of money was rather small—a little more than 700 *hiki* for the year—from the point of view of family history the estate was an important one. Encroachments by the local deputy had interrupted

5. For details, see H. Paul Varley and George Elison, "The Culture of Tea: From Its Origins to Sen no Rikyū," in George Elison and Bardwell L. Smith, eds., *Warlords, Artists, & Commoners: Japan in the Sixteenth Century* (Honolulu: The University Press of Hawaii, 1981).

6. The source of the comment is *Yamanoue sōjiki*. Quoted in Kidō Saizō, *Rengashi ronkō*, vol. 2 (Tokyo: Meiji Shoin, 1973), 651.

payment of revenues, it appears; Jōō had acted as intermediary and arranged for full payment. Furthermore, a similar incident occurred involving the revenue from the single biggest source of income for the Sanjōnishi house, the Aoso guild. If we look at Sanetaka's diary for the final days of 1530, we find Jōō turning over 3,000 *hiki* from that guild, and then adding 500 *hiki* later, making a total of 3,500 *hiki* in all. Finally, Jōō also sent Sanetaka a separate sum of 1,000 *hiki* on the last day of 1530. All of this was in payment for Sanetaka's services, which included a copy of the *Eiga taigai* text, criticism and correction of Jōō's poems, and replies to questions concerning literary matters.

In other words, in the case of Takeno Jōō we have a man who is referred to as a *rengashi* but who also belongs to category three (warriors and townsmen) and acts as a patron to a person in category one (the nobility). And it stands to reason that other townsmen fond of linked verse were powerful patrons not only for those in category one but also in category two, true *rengashi*.

An example substantiating this last contention is contained in *Seisuishō* ("Wakening Laughter," 1623), a much later and thus possibly unreliable text, and concerns the master Bontanka Shōhaku after he moved to Sakai in 1518.[7] The story is as follows:

> Annoyed by the large number of requests he was receiving for *hokku* ("first verses") commemorating the first month or the beginning of spring, Shōhaku had given his servant instructions to turn any requests away, begging illness as an excuse, and thus allowing himself rest. On the fifth day of the first month, however, the servant came in, even before Shōhaku had arisen for the day, to tell him that someone had come requesting a *hokku*. When Shōhaku scolded the servant, reminding him that he had ordered him to turn such requests away, the servant replied that the man was offering three *kanmon* for the poet's services. At this, Shōhaku jumped up out of bed and said, "Well, in that case I'll be happy to compose a verse!"[8]

The anecdote does not record who brought the three *kanmon* (300 *hiki*), but since the exchange took place in Sakai there is a strong possibility that the person was a wealthy townsmen with a taste for linked verse. The very fact that Shōhaku had moved to Sakai doubtless

7. A collection of anecdotes written by Anrakuan Sakuden (1554–1642).
8. Quoted in Shimazu, *Renga no kenkyū*, 306–7.

indicates that he already had patrons among the townsmen of that city—a fact that also lends some credibility to the story itself. At any rate, Sakai townsmen were important members of both categories three and four.

These examples involving Sanetaka, Jōō, and Shōhaku thus give us a fairly clear picture of the nature of patronage in late Muromachi Japan. Furthermore, the circumstances they portray also suggest the reason why professionalism developed first of all among masters of linked verse.

Looking at an overview of the categories will show that court nobles and professional masters of linked verse (categories one and two) were generally provided with financial and/or political support by townsmen, amateur devotees, and great warlords (categories three-five), the latter being the patrons of the world of linked verse. (Although the point will not be argued here, the men of category five are of course likely to emerge as primary patrons in any age and for any genre.) And the special characteristic that defines the relationships between categories one and two and between categories three and four is the presence of the master-disciple relationship.

The idea of the master-disciple relationship calls to mind the *iemoto* system that developed in the world of Japanese art. This system reached maturity in the eighteenth century, not in the Muromachi period. Its precursor, however, can be found in the world of linked verse.

The *iemoto* system is a system in which knowledge and training in an art form is transmitted only through designated houses or schools with "special knowledge" inherited from the past. Upon entering a course of discipline, some students forsake their own bloodline to become artistic heirs, with special privileges and duties. In time this would involve teaching new students—mostly amateurs who pay for their instruction. In a way, the system is thus like the esoteric schools of Buddhism, in which "secret teachings" and initiation rites are bestowed upon devotees who dedicate themselves to a semimystical "way" of life and learning. So characteristic is this mode of training to Japan that its pecularities are known wherever Japanese arts—the tea ceremony, flower arranging, and so forth—have been introduced.

Yet it is not the case that every kind of Japanese art has developed an *iemoto* system. For instance, there is an *iemoto* system in Noh drama, but none in Kabuki. The reason for this is that many people want to learn to chant Noh librettos and thus become amateur disciples. In Kabuki, however, fans enjoy the art but do not become disciples. In order for the *iemoto* system to develop, then, there must be a large number of amateur disciples with the considerable financial means necessary to support the artistic house. Another condition is that the house must have developed a complex and varied body of secret teachings concerning the form of the art, along with a system by which those teachings can be transmitted to disciples.

If linked verse is considered in terms of the above two conditions, it is quite possible that amateur disciples emerged very early in the history of the genre. Although it is difficult to fix the relationship between men in categories three and four as middle-ranking teachers and amateur disciples, there were probably many cases in which men in category four progressed into category three through study and practice. After all, the reason money passed from those in categories three and four to teachers in category one or masters in category two was because of special teachings received by the former from the latter. In order to make the results of these transmissions of knowledge appear special and esoteric, the organization of secret teachings was necessary—a development that had profound implications for the work of the masters of linked verse. It is common knowledge that Sōgi and later *rengashi* had a great deal to do with the so-called *Kokin denju*, or "*Kokinshū* Secret Traditions," which may be termed the very pinnacle of secret teachings. Those same *rengashi* were also instrumental in advancing the formation of the *kirigami denju* (secret teachings passed down from master to disciple in written form).[9] Moreover, we also know that Bontanka Shōhaku established the *Sakai denju*, who were responsible for the dissemination of poetic learning among the townsmen class.[10] That masters of linked verse not only taught their students how to compose linked verse but also became

9. The "secret teachings"—consisting mostly of anecdotal material, rules about pronunciation, and cautionary remarks—had been passed down orally within certain prominent noble families throughout the Kamakura and early Muromachi periods. During the fifteenth century the teachings were codified and began to circulate outside the boundaries of court culture as well.

10. The poet spent the last decade of his life in the port city of Sakai, where he attracted many students from the emerging merchant class.

associated with literary *denju* concerning *Genji monogatari* and other works may have been a feature of their lives incumbent upon them because of a profession that required them to rely so constantly on amateur disciples.

Of course, it may be argued that the same sort of situation also pertained in the world of *waka,* or formal court poetry in the *uta* form. However, I believe that the nature of linked verse as an art form is the reason the trend toward professionalism developed so conspicuously in linked verse. As has been pointed out, it was in the artistic nature of linked verse to seek its highest effects in the unity of feeling emerging from the members of the *za,* or group of participants in a linking session, thus placing emphasis on the immediate present of the group in a way different from the typical *uta* meeting. Furthermore, in the *renga* meeting, everyone participated in the composition of the poem in succession, with observers and observed alternating constantly. The amusement resulting from this—something lacking in court *uta*—made linked verse more popular among common people, with the result that *renga* was able to attract large numbers of amateur disciples.

In Japan, then, patterns of patronage differ depending on the nature of the art and the circumstances of the age. By looking carefully at the case of linked verse in the late Muromachi period, I have outlined the emergence of a new pattern of patronage, and I have ended with the hypothesis that in the Edo period that same pattern went on to give form to the foremost arts of Japan. In other words, Takeno Jōō, whether he knew it or not, brought into the world of tea a pattern of artistic existence that may have owed its basic definition less to the pages of *Eiga taigai* than to the art he had learned in his youth, the art of linked verse.

Saiokuken Sōchō and Imagawa Daimyo Patronage

H. Mack Horton

In the year 1519, Saiokuken Sōchō (1448–1532) was acclaimed the linked-verse poet "preeminent in all the realm" by the court noble and literatus Nakamikado Nobutane (1442–1525).[1] Although other contemporary *rengashi* such as Botanka Shōhaku (1443–1527) and Inawashiro Kensai (1452–1510) were no less esteemed as successors of the great Sōgi (1421–1502), there can be no doubt that by the latter decades of his long life, Sōchō was one of the best known and most respected figures in the linked-verse world during the golden age of that art. In those same years, Sōchō's patron, Imagawa Ujichika (ca. 1471–1526), was becoming one of the first *sengoku daimyō,* acquiring through military force and administrative fiat absolute primacy in Suruga and Tōtōmi provinces.[2] Befitting the house coming to be known as "the greatest warriors on the Eastern Seaboard" (*kaidō ichi no yumitori*), the Imagawa capital of Sunpu (modern Shizuoka City) began under Ujichika to develop into a provincial cultural center that

The author would like to thank Professors Kaneko Kinjirō, William and Helen McCullough, and Mary Elizabeth Berry for their contributions to this research and also the Fulbright Commission and the Japan Foundation for their generous support.

1. *Nobutanekyōki*: 1519.2.14, in vol. 22 of Takeuchi Rizō, ed., *Zoku shiryō taisei* (Rinsen Shoin, 1967), 232. Throughout the notes, the place of publication is Tokyo unless otherwise noted.
2. On the definition of *sengoku daimyō* and its applicability to Imagawa Ujichika, see Nagahara Keiji, *Sengoku no dōran,* vol. 14 of *Nihon no rekishi* (Shōgakukan, 1975), 51.

in its heyday would be rivaled only by that of the Ōuchi daimyo at Yamaguchi.

The history of the relationship between Sōchō and the Imagawa daimyo provides one valuable paradigm for understanding the nature of literary patronage in the Sengoku era. Sōchō not only served three generations of Imagawa leaders—Yoshitada (1436–76), Ujichika, and Ujiteru (1513–36)—but preserved a record of various aspects of his activities in their domain in five diaries, most importantly *Sōchō shuki* ("The Journal of Sōchō," 1522–27).[3] Those idiosyncratic yet vivid records, which are unmatched by even the voluminous diaries in Chinese (*kanbun*) for breadth of subject matter, not to mention degree of authorial presence, serve as the foundation of the following study.

The Cultural Heritage of the Imagawa House

When Sōchō was born in the town of Shimada in Suruga Province in 1448, the Imagawa had already been *shugo* (constables) of that province for over a century (see the abbreviated "Imagawa House Lineage," p. 161). Originally a branch of the Ashikaga family, the Imagawa had been awarded the constableship of Tōtōmi and then Suruga in the time of Imagawa Norikuni (1304–84) in recognition of his military exploits in the wars at the end of the Kenmu Restoration (1333), in which three of his brothers were killed. The Imagawa house was also known for its cultural attainments even in Norikuni's time. One famous anecdote relates that he rejected a request to contribute poetry to *Fugashu* ("Collection of Elegance," 1349), the seventeenth imperial *waka* anthology, modestly protesting that he composed verse only "to cultivate the spirit."[4] But in Norikuni's pursuit of excellence in both learning (*bun*) and battle (*bu*) he set an example later generations of Imagawa leaders would follow.

When Norikuni refused poetic honors, the anecdote continues, he directed his second son Sadayo (1325–1420) to contribute to the

3. Sōchō's five diaries are *Sōgi shūenki* (1502), *Azumaji no tsuto* (1509), *Utsunoyama no ki* (1518), *Sōchō shuki* (1522–27), and *Sōchō nikki* (1530–31). The text used here for *Sōchō shuki* (a later title) is Shimazu Tadao, *Sōchō nikki* (Iwanami Bunko, 1985), 7–143. All further references are noted in the text as SS. Versions of all but the last diary are also available in Shigematsu Hiromi, *Sōchō sakuhinshū, Koten bunko* 443 (1983).

4. *Ryōshun ben'yōshō,* in Hanawa Hokiichi, ed., *Gunsho ruijū,* vol. 16 (Zoku Gunsho Ruijū Kanseikai, 1959–60; 30 vols.), 434.

anthology instead. That son, better known in literary history as Imagawa Ryōshun, went on to become the greatest cultural figure the Imagawa were to produce. True to the *bun-bu* ideal, he spent years in Kyushu as Inspector (*tandai*), warring with the enemies of the bakufu, and he also held the constableship of Tōtōmi and, later, Suruga, while concurrently producing important literary works in a variety of genres. In poetry he studied with Reizei Tamehide (?–1372), one of the compilers of *Fūgashū,* and he was represented in that and several subsequent anthologies. Later generations of Imagawa leaders were to profit from the relationship Ryōshun fostered with the Reizei school. In linked verse he was instructed by Kyūsei (1282–?) and Nijō Yoshimoto (1320–88), compilers of the first imperially recognized *renga* anthology, *Tsukubashū* ("Tsukuba Collection," 1356–57). He wrote poetic treatises and may have been the author of a personal anthology of the first sixteen imperial poetry collections, *Nihachi meidai wakashū* ("Selections from the Sixteen Collections").[5] In prose, he produced travel works as well as *Nan taiheiki* ("A Critique of *Taiheiki,*" 1402), a critical study of the war tale *Taiheiki* ("The Great Peace," late fourteenth century) in which his own family figures. His written injunctions to his descendants, set forth in a document entitled *Imagawajō* ("Imagawa Code," 1394), were considered important enough to be included in the official chronicle of the house, *Imagawaki* ("Chronicle of the Imagawa"). *Imagawajō* became so famous that the name "Imagawa" was later used as a generic term for house injunctions.[6] In *Imagawajō,* he emphasized the importance of both *bun* and *bu* to the warrior leader: "Victory is unattainable without knowledge of the way of letters."[7] George Sansom summarizes the importance of Ryōshun's accomplishments and his seminal position in the history of the development of the poet-warrior:

5. The work is available in Mimura Terunori, ed., *Meidai waka zenshū* (Okayama: Fukutake Shoten, 1976). It is traditionally thought to have been compiled by Ryōshun, an attribution that no doubt contributed to Ujichika's decision to undertake a sequel (see p. 120).
6. *Imagawaki,* also called *Furokuki,* in Hanawa Hokiichi et al., eds., *Zoku gunsho ruijū,* vol. 21a (Zoku Gunsho Ruijū Kanseikai, 1957–72; 37 vols. with 3 supplements), 161–214. It includes a history of the house together with *Imagawajō, Fuji goran nikki, Kana mokuroku,* and a chart of the Imagawa daimyo lineage.
7. *Imagawajō,* in Ozawa Tomio, *Kakun* (Kodansha, 1985), 43–49, 238–42.

> It was remarkable that a member of the warrior class should have become a prominent figure in the literary society which had its centre at the Court. The very fact that he was accepted on terms of equality in such an exclusive group shows that a spirit of change was in the air, and a new model of warrior was coming into fashion.[8]

Ryōshun's example exerted a powerful influence on subsequent generations of Imagawa leaders, most notably Norimasa (1364–1433), considered a second exemplar of the *bun-bu* ethic by his own descendants. He studied poetry under Reizei Tamemasa (1361–1417), the son of Ryōshun's teacher, Tamehide, and had selections of his work included in the last imperial anthology, *Shin shokukokinshū* (1439). He was also acquainted with Ryōshun's student Seigan Shōtetsu (1381–1459) and Shōtetsu's disciple Shōkō (1412–94). Norimasa copied dozens of literary classics, and he authored a six-volume study of *Genji monogatari*.[9] In his old age, he was paid the signal honor of a visit by the shogun Ashikaga Yoshinori (1394-1441) and his literary retinue, including Asukai Masayo (1390-1452) and Gyōkō (1391-1455), compilers of *Shin shokukokinshū,* who both left poetic diaries of the trip.[10] A third extant poetic record of the event, *Fuji goran nikki* ("Diary of a Journey to Mount Fuji"), is very likely by Norimasa himself, and it too was included in *Imagawaki* as an inspiration to future Imagawa rulers.[11] Yoshinori's visit marks the beginning of the Suruga capital's development into a provincial cultural center. Norimasa is recorded in *Imagawaki* as having explicitly reiterated

8. George Sansom, *A History of Japan, 1334–1615* (Rutland, VT and Tokyo: Charles E. Tuttle, Co., 1974), 115.
9. *Genji monogatari teiyō,* 1432. See Imaga Keiji, ed., *Genji monogatari kochū shūsei* (Ōfūsha, 1979), vol. 2, 819–25. A list of works copied by Norimasa is found in Yonehara Masayoshi, *Sengoku bushi to bungei no kenkyū* (Ōfūsha, 1979), 819–25.
10. *Fuji kikō,* by Asukai Masayo and *Ran fujiki,* by Gyōkō. See Shirai Chūkō, *Chūsei no kikō bungaku* (Bunka Shobō Hakubunsha, 1976), 14–33.
11. See Shirai, *Chūsei no kikō bungaku,* 4–13. Kanō Masanobu (1434–1530), patriarch of the Kanō school of painters and originally in Norimasa's service, was ordered to paint a picture of Mount Fuji to commemorate Yorinori's stay. Akai Tatsurō, "Bijutsu kōgei no miyako," in Imaizumi Atsuo et al., eds., *Kinsei no taidō,* vol. 3 of *Kyōto no rekishi* (Gakugei Shorin, 1968), 639.

Ryōshun's commitment to the *bun-bu* ideal: "[*Imagawajō*] is the model for this house; truly it is an immutable guide for all time."[12]

But despite the house tradition for cultural accomplishment, Norimasa's eldest son Noritada (?–1461) was more immediately engaged by the question of succession. He finally triumphed in the house's first internal power struggle, the Eikyō Era Succession Conflict (*Eikyō no naikō*) of 1432 to 1433, and thereafter distinguished himself more by military than cultural activity, first against disaffected local warlords (*kokujin*) in his own domain, then on the side of the shogun against his renegade deputy in Kamakura in the Eikyō Era Discord (*Eikyō no ran*) of 1438. Nevertheless, he too found time for literary pursuits, and Sōchō speaks in *Sōchō shuki* of finding poetry composed by Noritada for the thirty-third anniversary of Ryōshun's death (SS, 134).

Noritada's son Yoshitada, with whom Sōchō's involvement in Imagawa affairs began, peacefully succeeded to the headship of the house two months before Noritada died. With Suruga firmly under his control, Yoshitada devoted his energies to the recovery of Imagawa influence in Tōtōmi, which had been transferred to the constableship of the Shiba family in the early fifteenth century. Yoshitada's campaign against the Shiba house and its allies in that province was the focal point of his last years, and it forms the background of the early history of Sōchō.[13]

Sōchō and Imagawa Yoshitada

Sōchō (as he later called himself) is thought to have been a younger son of Gojō Yoshisuke, founder of a renowned family of

12. *Imagawaki* (*Furokuki*) in *Zoku gunsho ruijū*, vol. 21a, 184.
13. For more background on Sōchō's life, see Donald Keene, "The Comic Tradition in Renga," in John W. Hall and Toyoda Takeshi, eds., *Japan in the Muromachi Age* (Berkeley, Los Angeles, and London: University of California Press, 1977), 241–77, and "Sōchō," in *Some Japanese Portraits* (Tokyo, New York, and San Francisco: Kōdansha, 1978), 27–34. For Sōchō's chronology, see Ōshima Toshiko, "Sōchō nenpu," *Joshidai bungaku* 24 (February 1962): 38–54. Ōshima has also compiled a guide to Sōchō's associates: "Sōchō no shūhen," *Joshidai bungaku* 28 (February 1963): 28–40; no.32 (February 1964): 29–33; no.33 (May 1964): 20–28, and no.35 (October 1964): 76–85.

swordsmiths in Shimada, Sōchō's birthplace.[14] Yoshisuke was in the service of Yoshitada, who is thought to have granted him the use of the *yoshi* character of his own name as a mark of favor.[15] The young Sōchō was thus in a position to meet the warrior elite of the domain. At the relatively late age of seventeen, however, he entered the Buddhist priesthood, eventually taking ordination (*jukai*), preparatory discipline (*kegyō*), and baptism (*kanjō*) in the Shingon sect. He thus had considerably more religious training than most *rengashi,* who often donned religious garb *pro forma* and called themselves *hōshi* (priest). But instead of retreating into a monastery, Sōchō thereafter accompanied Yoshitada's army, probably as a monk-scribe (*shokisō*). In his *Utsunoyama no ki* ("Utsunoyama Diary," 1518), a travel diary cum autobiography, Sōchō wrote that he campaigned with Yoshitada and "mingled with the dust of encampments."[16] Thus, even his early years were marked by a combination of secular and

14. Saitō Kiyoe, in his "Rengashi Sōchō nenpu tsuikō," in Hisamatsu Sen'ichi, ed., *Nihon bungei no sekai* (Ōfūsha, 1968), 251, says Sōchō was the third son, as does Ijichi Tetsuo, "Sōchō den kōsetsu," *Renga to haikai* 4 (November 1936): 15. Takakura Yoshiaki, in a more recent and better documented study entitled "Imagawashi to Shimada kaji," in Imagawashi Kenkyūkai, ed., *Suruga no Imagawashi* (Shizuoka City: Yashimaya, 1986), vol. 9, 104, says he was the second son. Ōtsuka Isao, in a recent revisionist study of Sōchō's early years, points out that there was also a line of swordsmiths located in Shimada who used the name Munenaga (written with the same characters as "Sōchō") in the Sengoku and Edo periods. He speculates therefore that the belief that Sōchō's forebears worked in that profession may have been the result of an early conflation and thus not true. Ōtsuka cites as supporting evidence the fact that Sōchō makes no mention of Shimada in *Sōchō shuki* although he passes through it four times during the years covered therein. See Ōtsuka Isao, "Rengashi Sōchō no wakaki koro," in Imagawashi Kenkyūkai, *Suruga no Imagawashi,* vol. 9, 168–75. But Sōchō's own characteristically modest testimony in his journal *Utsuyama no ki* that he was "the child of a humble artisan of little skill," together with the fact that the notion of swordsmith antecedents was already well established in the early Edo period, lends support to the standard biography, and Ōtsuka presents his findings only as an alternate hypothesis worthy of further investigation. See Sōchō, *Utsuyama no ki,* in *Gunsho ruijū,* vol. 17, 404.

15. Takakura, "Imagawashi to Shimada kaji," 99–132.

16. *Utsunoyama no ki,* 404. This section is translated in Keene, "The Comic Tradition," 261–62. Further references to previously untranslated sections of *Utsunoyama no ki* appear in the text as UYK.

sacred influences that would have a profound impact on his entire career. Traveling with Yoshitada's army gave him a firsthand appreciation of the military affairs he would later chronicle for the Imagawa and for their vassals, the Asahina.

In his old age, Sōchō composed a document that he included in *Sōchō shuki* outlining his lifelong relationship with the Imagawa house. Although he devoted most of his remarks to Ujichika and Ujiteru, his lines on Yoshitada give further hints as to the nature of their relationship. He wrote, "Although I was in no special service to Lord Yoshitada, I was close to him day and night for years" (SS, 135). The sentence shows that while Sōchō had become a monk and thus was not an official retainer of Yoshitada, he enjoyed personal ties with the daimyo. Ijichi Tetsuo theorizes about a homosexual relationship as well.[17]

In the tradition of his forebears, Yoshitada also found time for literary pursuits, but in a more limited way than Ryōshun or Norimasa. According to *Imagawa ryakki* ("Abbreviated Chronicle of the Imagawa"), "He was a spirited and courageous general, accomplished with both bow and horse. He also appreciated *waka* and *renga*."[18] *Imagawa keizu* ("Imagawa Lineage") adds, "He enjoyed *renga* and studied with the priest Sōgi."[19] These encomia of Yoshitada's literary interests were perhaps exaggerated, but it is true that Sōgi's first collection of personal verses, *Wasuregusa* ("Grass of Forgetfulness," 1474), includes lines the poet composed at Yoshitada's manor in 1466. During Sōgi's stay, Sōchō, then eighteen, took advantage of his Imagawa ties to invite the elder poet to one of Suruga's most famous poetic spots (*uta-makura*), Kiyomi Strand, thus beginning a relationship that was to last until Sōgi's death thirty-six years later. It was also Sōchō's first step away from the status of a mere provincial to a national figure.

Seven years later, in 1473, Sōchō acted as a guide for another famous poet, Shōkō, who had come to visit Yoshitada. Shōkō's teacher Shōtetsu had studied with Imagawa Ryōshun, and both Shōtetsu and Shōkō had been acquainted with Imagawa Norimasa. Shōkō's call on Yoshitada thus had a personal aspect that is reflected in Sōchō's account of the visit in *Sōchō shuki*:

17. Ijichi, "Sōchō den kōsetsu," 14–25.
18. *Imagawake ryakki,* in Yonehara, *Sengoku bushi to bungei no kenkyū,* 830.
19. *Imagawa keizu,* in Yonehara, *Sengoku bushi to bungei no kenkyū,* 830.

Shōkō too came down to Suruga years ago. I invited him to Kiyomi Strand as well and had us rowed about Mihogasaki. On the return he composed this:

Under the moonlight,
for how many ages have
the waves rolled in on
Kiyomi Strand and ravaged
the fence at the gate?

tsuki nagara / iku yo no nami o / kiyomigata / yosete zo arasu / seki no aragaki

He wrote it on a fence post of Kiyomi Gate. Now even that has completely rotted away. . . .

Shōkō thereafter desired to have a part of the fence made into a box for poem strips [*tanzakubako*], and soon Lord Yoshitada ordered it done and sent off. Shōkō also asked him to include one of his own compositions:

Say that you were there
to all in the capital—
this will bear witness,
from the rude fence of the gate
at the Strand of Kiyomi.

tazunetsu to / miyako ni katare / kiyomigata / kore zo shirushi no / seki no aragaki

Shōkō had this poem lacquered in *maki-e* on the lid and treasured it. (SS, 49-50)[20]

Yoshitada thus subscribed to Ryōshun's teachings and devoted himself both to expanding his domain and to hosting poets and

20. Shōkō records the episode in his *Shōkō nikki,* in *Gunsho ruijū,* vol. 18, 646, as follows:

On the nineteenth Lord Yoshitada sent me a piece of the fence at Kiyomi Gate along with this poem:

Say that you were there
to all in the capital—
this is a true piece
from the rude fence of the gate
at the Strand of Kiyomi.

tazunetsu to / miyako ni katare / kiyomigata / kore zo makoto no / seki no aragaki

encouraging literary pursuits. Sōchō, despite his youth, contributed to the literary life at Yoshitada's capital, while no doubt profiting from contact with prominent poets of the period.

Yoshitada also contributed to the incipient cultural efflorescence of the Imagawa capital through his marriage to the niece of Ise Sadachika (1417–73), advisor to the shogun, Ashikaga Yoshimasa (1435–90). The marriage is thought to have taken place in 1467, when Yoshitada was in Kyoto to reinforce Hosokawa Katsumoto (1430–73) and the Eastern Army at the start of the Ōnin War (1467–77).[21] Sōchō may have accompanied him.[22] The marriage gave Yoshitada a closer connection to the highest reaches of the warrior aristocracy and, by extension, to members of the court. The Kyoto acquaintances of his wife, who was later known as Lady Kitagawa (ca. 1442-1529) from the location of her home in the Suruga capital, were later instrumental in arranging for the marriage of Kitamuki, the daughter of Lady Kitagawa and Yoshitada, to the court aristocrat Ōgimachisanjō Sanemochi (1463–1530). Sanemochi became one of Sōchō's close friends. Lady Kitagawa herself was a lifelong supporter of Sōchō, and she will figure further on in this study. For Yoshitada, his marriage was the nuptial equivalent of both *bun* and *bu,* for Lady Kitagawa's elder brother was the warrior later known as Hōjō Sōun (1432–1519), who would become master of Izu and Sagami provinces. The marriage gave Yoshitada a military ally whose subsequent contributions to Imagawa fortunes were manifold, while also drawing him closer to the cultural world of

---

I had wanted to take a piece of the fence and make a box for poem strips out of it, but I had refrained, as I was afraid people would say I had stolen it. The gift pleased me very much. My reply:

> It is not a person
> but pinewood that brings word
> to the capital
> from the rude fence of the gate
> at the Strand of Kiyomi.
>
> hito narade / miyako no tsuto zo / kiyomigata /
> seki no aragaki / matsu no koto no ha

21. Owada Tetsuo et al., *Shizuokashi shi: genshi, kodai, chūsei,* (Shizuoka City: Shizuoka Shiyakusho, 1981), 987.
22. Ōshima, "Sōchō nenpu."

the capital. It represents a further step in the incorporation of Kyoto culture that was to advance so much under subsequent Imagawa daimyo.

Sōchō and Imagawa Ujichika

Yoshitada's desire to regain the province of Tōtōmi had fatal consequences, for he was killed there in 1476 in battle with local warlords loyal to the Shiba house. His death in his prime brought about another succession dispute (*Bunmei no naikō*), this one between forces loyal to his five-year-old son Ryūōmaro (later Ujichika) and those supporting a more mature candidate, Oga Norimitsu, a cousin of Yoshitada.[23] Lady Kitagawa went into hiding with her son at the home of Hasegawa Masanobu (1430–1516) and relied on her brother Sōun to bring about a settlement between the forces of the disputants and their respective allies from two rival branches of the Uesugi family, who each hoped to profit by the conflict at the expense of the other. Sōun brought about an agreement between the two sides, wherein Norimitsu would serve as interim head of the Imagawa house until Ryūōmaro attained his majority, and in 1478 Sōun obtained a guarantee from the shogun to that effect.

The crisis averted, Norimitsu installed himself in the Suruga capital, and Lady Kitagawa and her son took up residence in the post town of Mariko where they lived for ten years. Sōchō was later to make Mariko the site of his own hermitage. But Ryūōmaro's fifteenth year came and went with no indication that the interim leader would relinquish his position. By 1487 the young heir could wait no longer; with Sōun's help he attacked Norimitsu, killed him, and took over command of the Imagawa domain. He assumed the name Ujichika on the occasion of his belated coming-of-age ceremony, then in the following years he worked to realize his father's ambitions in Tōtōmi with the aid of Sōun, while alternately supporting Sōun's forays into the Kantō.[24]

23. The exact date of Ujichika's birth is unsettled, with the dates 1490, 1491, and 1493 proposed. Owada Tetsuo argues in favor of 1471. See Owada Tetsuo, *Suruga Imagawa ichizoku* (Shinjinbutsu Ōraisha, 1983), 142. Ryūōmaro is alternatively read Tatsuōmaro.

24. On the campaigns of Ujichika and Sōun in Tōtōmi and the Kantō, see Akimoto Taiji, "Imagawa Ujichika no Tōtōmi keiryaku," in Arimitsu Yūgaku, ed., *Imagawashi no kenkyū*, vol. 11 of *Sengoku daimyō ronshū* (Yoshikawa Kōbunkan, 1984), 113–35.

Sōchō, for his part, had on the death of Yoshitada left Suruga to begin his literary apprenticeship with Sōgi in the capital. He also accompanied his teacher on journeys to the domains of culturally inclined daimyo, acquiring valuable personal connections as well as experience in the profession of traveling linked-verse poet. It was also in those years in the capital that Sōchō met and studied with the great Zen prelate Ikkyū Sōjun (1394–1481), whose influence on Sōchō's spiritual development was as pervasive as Sōgi's influence on his literary art.[25]

According to extant records, Sōchō did not return to Suruga until 1496, twenty years after his departure for the Kansai.[26] One scholar assumes it was the artistic reputation Sōchō achieved during the intervening decades that enabled him to return to the Imagawa domain and acquire the patronage of Ujichika, the son of his earlier protector.[27] By 1496 Sōchō had indeed become one of the most important *renga* poets in the country, having participated in the composition of such linked-verse sequences as *Minase sangin* ("Three Poets at Minase," 1488) and *Yuyama sangin* ("Three Poets at Yuyama," 1491) and having had more than three dozen verses selected for inclusion in the second imperially recognized *renga* anthology, *Shinsen tsukubashū* ("The New Tsukuba Collection," 1495). He had also authored several guides to poetic study.

Sōchō does not mention any return to Suruga before this time in the *Utsunoyama no ki,* but he seems to imply such activity in the passage in *Sōchō shuki* cited earlier in reference to his relationship with Yoshitada. Sōchō writes:

> When Ujichika was a child, I took my leave to go to Daitokuji. He showed me great consideration. For twenty years I came and went from the capital and enjoyed his special favor. Everyone must know that. Moreover, from time to time I was of service to him. (SS, 136)

25. On Sōchō's relationship with Ikkyū, see Nakamoto Tamaki, "Ikkyū Sōjun to Saiokuken Sōchō," in *Renga to sono shūhen: Kaneko Kinjirō Hakase kanreki kinen ronbunshū* (Hiroshima Chūsei Bungei Kenkyūkai, 1967), 254–71.
26. Ōshima, "Sōchō nenpu."
27. Kidō Saizō, "Sengoku shoki ni okeru rengashi no seikatsu—Sōchō, Shōhaku, Sōseki no baai," *Bungaku* 40.10 (October 1972): 75.

It thus appears that Sōchō kept in touch periodically with Lady Kitagawa and Ryūōmaro (Ujichika) at Mariko and then at the Suruga capital during those two formative decades, and perhaps, although there is as yet no proof, he kept Ujichika apprised of events in the capital and in the domains of the daimyo he visited with Sōgi. It is difficult to justify Sōchō's remark that he received Ujichika's special favor if they were not in at least occasional contact.

Sōchō's testimony also suggests that his relationship with the Imagawa did change in nature after two decades had passed. That is underscored by his account of this period in the *Utsunoyama no ki*:

> After I returned to Suruga, violence broke out in Kyoto, and the cottage I had lived in there was burned. I went back to the capital only to return here, where I built a house near Ujichika. I planted spring and autumn trees and other flora, made a large pond, and brought in abundant fresh water. I was blessed with a plentiful crop of rice to tide me over summer and winter, and the smoke from my cooking fire rose morning and evening. (UYK, 396)

It appears, then, that whether or not Sōchō had maintained interim contact, he decided at some point in the latter 1490s to acquire a more permanent base in the Imagawa capital. Ikkyū was dead, Sōchō was well known and already about fifty years old, and Suruga held the promise of relative tranquility and Imagawa support.[28]

After Sōchō established what he called his "residence by the river," he continued to travel back and forth to Kyoto but also began to take part in the poetic and literary life of the Imagawa capital.[29] One early record shows he was ordered by Ujichika in the ninth month of 1503 to conduct a *renga* session in celebration of the building of Kaichōji in Shimizu.[30] Before many more years had passed, Sōchō

28. The *rengashi* Kensai was likewise about fifty when he abandoned his career in the capital for a hermitage in the east. See Kaneko Kinjirō, *Rengashi kensai denkō*, rev. ed. (Ōfūsha, 1977), 157.

29. Sōchō's "residence by the river" (*kawabe no shukusho* [SS, 52] or *kawara chikaki shukusho* [SS, 53]), probably named Rinsen'an, later became Sōchōji temple. See Nakagawa Yoshio, "Rengashi Sōchō," in Owada, *Shizuokashi shi*, 1310–19.

30. Kurosawa Osamu, "Zōzenjidono Kyōzan Jōki Daizenjōmon Imagawa Ujichika nenpyō," in Imagawashi Kenkyūkai, *Suruga no Imagawashi*, vol. 1 (1975), 159–79.

was confident enough of his place among the Imagawa and their retainers to request that a second, more rustic residence, his "Brushwood Cottage" (Saioku), be built for him in Mariko on the fief of an important Imagawa vassal, Saitō Yasumoto.[31] Sōchō wrote in retrospect of the project in *Utsunoyama no ki*:

> At the beginning of the Eishō era [1504–22], I decided I wanted to build this mountain cottage and so spoke to Yasumoto. It was quite easily done. That spring at the beginning of the third month, I composed this *hokku* for a linked-verse session at Yasumoto's:
>
> The mountain cherries—
> how my longing for them is
> enhanced by the haze!
>
> yamazakura / omou iro sou / kasumi kana
>
> By this I meant that I felt my desire for a mountain cottage would be fulfilled and that the haze on the peak and the mountain scenery made me anticipate it all the more. In the fourth month we selected a spot and built the cottage in the usual way. (UYK, 396)

This and the earlier passage from the *Utsunoyama no ki* show that Sōchō enjoyed comfortable accommodations in Mariko in addition to his house in the Suruga capital, and that he had enough land and help to grow abundant rice for his own consumption. He also had servants, and later he was to have two children by, as he referred to her, "the woman who did my clothes" (UYK, 404).

At the same time that Sōchō was becoming established in Ujichika's capital, the daimyo himself was restoring Tōtōmi to Imagawa rule and solidifying his direct personal control over his lands and retainers. His regime, which spanned four decades, initiated a renaissance of Imagawa influence and fully established the Imagawa capital as an important provincial center.

31. The traditional date given for the construction of Sōchō's cottage in Mariko is 1504, based on the phrase "At the beginning of the Eishō era [1504–22]" in *Utsunoyama no ki*. Shigematsu Hiromi, however, argues the date was actually 1506. See Shigematsu Hiromi, "Saiokuken ketsuan nenji shiron," *Renga haikai kenkyū* 56 (January 1979): 9–19.

Ujichika's conquest of Tōtōmi began in earnest after he was granted land in the province by the bakufu in 1493. Like his father, Yoshitada, he met stiff opposition from the Shiba house and its allies among the local warlords but was nevertheless appointed constable in 1508. He finally crushed the last Shiba resistance in 1517 at Hikuma Castle. He also made substantial inroads into Mikawa Province. Sōchō was with Ujichika on some of his campaigns as he had been with Ujichika's father, and his account of Ujichika's crossing of the Tenryū River and the siege of Hikuma show the Imagawa general's engineering skill and his army's brutality, as well as Sōchō's role as chronicler and *renga* master:

> There was a flood at the time and the Tenryū River was like a great sea. Ujichika built a pontoon bridge with three hundred or more boats lashed together with ten or twenty great bamboo ropes. It was as the ground itself. I made a thousand verses in prayer for a safe crossing. The *hokku*:
>
> The Waterless Month—
> no victor who does not cross on foot,
> as there are no waves.
>
> minazuki / kachibito naranu / seze mo nashi
>
> It now occurs to me I ought to have said, "a crossing made by victors, / all of them on foot" (*mina kachibito no / watari kana*).
>
> The enemy came out on the far side of the river, and their arrows fell like rain. Tens of thousands of Imagawa troops crossed easily, and the foe pulled back. Ujichika encircled their castle with troops six or seven rows deep, covering an area of more than fifty *chō*. There, from the sixth through the eighth month, he harassed them. The soldiers in the last stronghold, Hikuma, resisted for several days and then capitulated on the nineteenth of the eighth month. Ujichika used men from the Abeyama gold mines to undermine the well in the fortress, and there was not a drop of water to be had inside. The Ōuchi—brothers, fathers, and sons—the Ōmi, the Takahashi, and the others in the castle with them were either killed, left for dead, or taken prisoner. The fleeing men and women were a pitiful sight. (SS, 11–12)

The above account is part of Sōchō's chronicle of the Asahina family, vassals of the Imagawa, that Sōchō appended to his *Sōchō shuki* (SS, 8–14). It, plus another house history, *Imagawa kafu* ("Record of the Imagawa House"), which he reworked into *kana*, have long been among the basic sources of information on Ujichika's Tōtōmi campaigns.[32]

What Ujichika gained by the sword, he worked equally hard to consolidate through administrative measures, including cadastral surveys (*kenchi*), beginning as early as 1518.[33] His activities constituted a wholesale reorganization of the previous pattern of land tenure and an assertion of Imagawa hegemony over land proprietorship. Ujichika sought as well to exercise similar control over the local landholders themselves and make them direct Imagawa vassals; in the last year of his life he promulgated *Imagawa kana mokuroku* ("*Kana* Precepts of the Imagawa") to codify and perpetuate this system for his descendants.[34] Nagahara Keiji has called the code the first mature Sengoku-era house laws (*kahō*).[35] The cadastral surveys and house laws signified a renunciation of the subordinate role of bakufu constable. The Imagawa were among the few *shugo daimyō* to successfully accomplish this shift to *sengoku daimyō* status.

In working to assume broad personal control over an independent domain, Ujichika was in effect fashioning a principality of a kind, with himself as its sovereign.[36] As cultural accomplishments had gone hand in hand with political power since the early days of the Japanese court, it behooved Ujichika as well to pursue cultural activi-

32. *Imagawa kafu,* in *Zoku gunsho ruijū,* vol. 21a, 141–60. A variant text of *Imagawa kafu* is included in a second *Imagawaki,* in *Zoku gunsho ruijū,* vol. 21a, 216–51, together with a house lineage, *Fuji goran nikki,* and miscellaneous addenda. It is not to be confused with the *Imagawaki* that is also known as *Furokuki* (see n. 6 above), which includes a more detailed history of the Imagawa but only up to the violence surrounding Ujichika's succession in ca. 1487–88.
33. For more on Ujichika's *kenchi* and other administrative policies, see Owada Tetsuo, "Imagawa Ujichika to sono monjo," in Arimitsu, *Imagawashi no kenkyū,* 94–112.
34. For a study of this document and its importance, see Ozawa Seichi, "*Imagawa kana mokuroku* no kaidoku," in Imagawashi Kenkyūkai, *Suruga no Imagawashi,* vol. 1, 29–35, and Matsudaira Norimichi, "*Imagawa kana mokuroku,*" also in *Suruga no Imagawashi,* vol. 1, 36–48.
35. Nagahara, *Sengoku no dōran,* 52–53.
36. I have borrowed this concept from Peter Judd Arnesen, *The Medieval Japanese Daimyo: The Ōuchi Family's Rule of Suō and Nagato* (New Haven and London: Yale University Press, 1979), 194.

ties consonant with his princely status, and in so doing acquire greater grandeur and legitimacy in the eyes of his vassals. This he did with dedication, carrying on a rich, personal literary life and fostering the cultural development of his capital, formally named Sunpu in about 1520, on the model of Kyoto. *Imagawa kafu* states that "Although the way of poetry had been followed by generations of Imagawa leaders, Ujichika was particularly gifted in such pursuits and was also skilled in strategy, horsemanship, and swimming."[37] Just as he had brought about a revival of Imagawa political fortunes, Ujichika worked to effect a literary renaissance, with Ryōshun and Norimasa as his models. He is said to have kept by his side a copy of *Nihachi meidai wakashū*, attributed to Ryōshun, and later he personally compiled a sequel to it, *Shokugo meidai wakashū* ("Selections from the Five Later Collections," 1516), to cover the last imperial anthologies. He was aided in this work by Sōjun, son of Tō no Tsuneyori (1401–ca. 1484), the latter having instructed Sōgi in the "*Kokinshū* Secret Traditions" (*Kokin denju*). The Tō school of poetry would not have survived without Imagawa support. Ujichika also relied on the great court literatus Sanjōnishi Sanetaka (1455–1537) for advice on poetry. He was, in addition, an avid student of *Taiheiki* and Ryōshun's *Nan taiheiki*, and he asked Nakamikado Nobutane to prepare for him a selection of the places in *Taiheiki* related to the Imagawa.[38] And of course Ujichika composed *renga* from time to time in Sōchō's company.

The development of Ujichika's domain into a cultural center was further stimulated by fostering additional ties with courtiers from Kyoto, partly through the agency of Ujichika's mother, Lady Kitagawa. One such aristocrat was Ujichika's own wife, best known by the name Jukei (ca. 1490–1568), which she took upon taking holy orders after Ujichika's death.[39] She was the daughter of the courtier Nakamikado Nobutane, whose connection with the Imagawa went back to the time of Norimasa, from whom he had received the secret traditions of *Man'yōshū*.[40] This relationship and the marriage of Ujichika's sister Kitamuki to Ōgimachisanjō Sanemochi were no doubt instrumental in effecting Ujichika's union with Jukei, probably in

37. *Imagawa kafu*, 154–55.
38. Yonehara, *Sengoku bushi to bungei no kenkyū*, 840.
39. For an early review of Jukei's life, see Adachi Shūtarō, *Imagawa Ujichika to Jukeini* (Shizuoka City: Yashimaya, 1931).
40. Owada, *Shizuokashi shi*, 1208

1505.[41] Like Ujichika, Jukei made literary requests of Sanetaka through her father Nobutane. It was probably through this route, and not via Sōchō, that Ujichika and Sanetaka began corresponding, though Sōchō became involved soon after.[42]

The courtly in-laws of Ujichika and Kitamuki naturally began to look to Suruga for support in a time when their own lands were being wrested from their control. Ōgimachisanjō Sanemochi, his son Kin'e (1494–1578), and Nakamikado Nobutane's son Nobuhide (1469–1531) all stayed in the Imagawa capital during Ujichika's lifetime. Sanemochi resided there for twenty-one years, and Kin'e, for twenty-three. Reizei Tamekazu (1486–1549), who held lands in the domain and lived in Sunpu almost continually from 1531 to 1548 or 1549, may have visited while Ujichika was alive as well.[43] Ujichika in turn welcomed those relationships, despite the drain on his finances they entailed, such as a gift of ten thousand *hiki* in "travel money" (*rosen*) to enable Kin'e to make the journey east to his domain.[44] Those nobles further contributed to the cultural renown of the Imagawa house, and all but Tamekazu figure in *Sōchō shuki.*

But in his personal cultural pursuits, Ujichika relied heavily on Sōchō, and the linked-verse master served Ujichika in a variety of ways. His most important official function was the composition of votive (*hōraku*) *renga,* sometimes on military campaigns with Ujichika and sometimes in the Suruga capital. Votive *uta* and *renga* were composed in supplication or gratitude to Shinto and Buddhist deities in recognition of the power of poetry to "effortlessly move heaven

41. Owada suggests the marriage took place in 1505 or 1508 (*Suruga Imagawa ichizoku,* 160). Yonehara thinks it was the former (*Sengoku bushi to bungei no kenkyū,* 842).
42. Yonehara, *Sengoku bushi to bungei no kenkyū,* 842–43.
43. Yonehara (*Sengoku bushi to bungei no kenkyū,* 902) cites an entry in the *Sanetakakōki* stating that Tamekazu was in Suruga in 1510, but Ujichika is not mentioned. Semoto Hisao, however, holds that Tamekazu arrived in Sunpu in 1529, a year not covered in *Sōchō shuki* or *Sōchō nikki* and three years after Ujichika's death. See Semoto Hisao, "Reizei Tamekazu to Imagawa Ujiteru, Yoshimoto," in Imagawashi Kenkyūkai, *Suruga no Imagawashi,* vol. 6 (1982), 138. Semoto says Tamekazu remained there until 1549, but Yonehara gives the date as 1548.
44. Owada, *Shizuokashi shi,* 1218. The *hiki* was a theoretical unit of value equal to ten copper cash (*mon*) or .86 *shō* (1.5 liters of rice) in 1522, according to *Dokushi biyō*; 100 *shō* equaled one *koku*. Its actual value, however, differed by region.

and earth and mollify unseen spirits and gods," as expounded in the *Kokinshū* preface.[45] Sōchō composed several such sequences for Ujichika, such as the one quoted earlier that he made for a successful crossing of the Tenryū River. The famous *Shutsujin senku* ("A Thousand Verses for the Campaign") was another of this variety, made after a great victory by Ujichika and Sōun in the Kantō in 1504 (SS, 9–10). Votive verses were also made before battles, for it was believed that they could bring about success.[46] But their efficacy was also related to poetic skill, and Sōchō was forced to compose the thousand verses of *Shutsujin senku* himself, in the absence of other talented poets.[47] Sōchō also made votive verses at the direction of Ujichika for nonmilitary purposes, the sequence for the construction of a temple at Shimizu being one example. Another well-known thousand-verse sequence, *Sengen senku* ("A Thousand Verses for Sengen Shrine," 1514), was an apotropaic composition to protect Ujichika during a *yakudoshi,* a year thought particularly dangerous for him. There were votive verses for the repose of the dead as well, one example being *Jukkai hyakuin dokugin* ("One Hundred Verses Alone, in Lamentation"), which Sōchō composed for the benefit of the deceased Imagawa vassal Asahina Yasuhiro.[48] The earliest known literary encounter between Sōchō and Ujichika also involved an informal votive composition of this sort after the death of Sōgi in 1502. Sōchō's record of the event in his *Sōgi shūenki* ("The Death of Sōgi") also gives a sense of the nature of his early relationship with Ujichika:

> On the night of the fifteenth [of the eighth month, 1502] a linked-verse session was held at the constable's residence. One of our number related that Sōgi had planned to be in Suruga at the time of the full moon, and that he had had difficulty preparing an appropriate *hokku* for the occasion. As Sōgi labored to compose the verse, a person accompany-

45. On the various types of votive verses see Fukui Kyūzō, *Renga no shiteki kenkyū* (Yūseidō, 1959), 24–78, and on the religious aspects of thousand-verse sequences, see Shimazu Tadao, "Senku renga kōgyō to sono hensen," in *Renga no kenkyū* (Kadokawa Shoten, 1973), 109–21.
46. Yamada Yoshio, *Renga gaisetsu* (Iwanami Shoten, 1937), 196.
47. See Sōchō's postscript to the *Shutsujin senku* in *Zoku gunsho ruijū,* vol. 17a, 564. Harada Yoshioki suggests that it was Sōchō, not Ujichika, who initiated the sequence. Harada Yoshioki, *Tankyū Nihon bungaku, chūko chūsei hen* (Kasama Shobō, 1979), 338.
48. *Jukkai hyakuin dokugin,* in Ijichi Tetsuo, ed., *Renga hyakuinshū* (Kyūko Shoin, 1975), 244–48.

ing him observed that on the same night of the full moon in the autumn of the previous year in Echigo the master had made two *hokku* for a linked-verse session and that one had been left over. Sōgi had thereupon decided to use the second in Suruga.

On hearing this, we took that verse as our *hokku* that evening:

Do not cloud over,
for you alone will be blamed,
full moon of autumn.
Sōgi

kumoru na yo / taga na wa tataji / aki no tsuki

Their calls make clear the number
of the geese that course the sky.
(Constable) Ujichika

sora tobu kari no / kazu shiruki koe

A cold morning dew
on the field of bush clover
in the wending wind.
Sōchō

kohagihara / asatsuyu samumi / kaze sugite

During a session with fixed topics that same night, on "Under the moon, longing for an old friend" the constable composed this:

I reflect upon
this autumn when he became
a man of old and
left behind the evening moon
we would have viewed together.
Ujichika

tomo ni min / tsuki no koyoi no / nokoshiokite /
furubito to naru/ aki o shi zo omou

Might this mean that although he waits for Sōgi, he does so in vain?

. . . We continued late into the night, composing the hundred verses as we spoke of various things from last year and this, around a flame that gave scant comfort.[49]

49. *Sōgi shūenki,* in Kaneko Kinjirō, *Sōgi tabi no ki shichū* (Ōfūsha, 1976), 119–20.

Ujichika composed poetry at the session with Sōchō and Sōseki (1474–1533) and shared his grief with them at Sōgi's loss. But he contributed only one of the hundred verses of the sequence, leaving the rest to the two *renga* masters.

Sōchō also conducted *renga* sessions not of a votive nature in Sunpu at the behest of the Imagawa, and he exchanged *waka* with them as well. Examples of such poems will be discussed presently. Although his diaries make no mention of it, Sōchō most likely also tutored Ujichika in his poetic study.

Sōchō's services for Ujichika were by no means limited to *renga* sessions. We have already observed, for example, that he composed the chronicle of the Asahina family and rewrote *Imagawa kafu* into *kana*. He also composed in or after 1528 a postscript for *Fuji goran nikki*, the travel diary attributed to Norimasa. No section of Sōchō's diaries explicitly refers to such activities, but the large number of humorous stories and comic poetry in *Sōchō shuki* and *Sōchō nikki* ("The Diary of Sōchō") suggests that he, like many other *rengashi*, also recounted amusing anecdotes for Ujichika and his immediate retainers, especially when on military campaigns.[50] Sōchō was a jack of all literary trades for Ujichika, especially in the first part of their relationship, and he served the daimyo in much the same way that the *dōbōshū* served the Ashikaga shogun.

Sōchō also performed literary services for Ujichika when traveling. Despite his permanent residences in Suruga, Sōchō spent a large part of his last thirty years visiting the domains of other daimyo or local warlords who were anxious for the chance to improve their *renga* skill under the direction of a first-rate linked-verse master.[51] Sōchō also spent much time at temples affiliated with Daitokuji, which was associated with his late mentor, Ikkyū, and he made fund-raising trips for that temple as well. While on those journeys, Sōchō also served on occasion as a messenger for Ujichika to court nobles in Kyoto, particularly to Sanjōnishi Sanetaka, whom Sōchō first met in about 1485. The first reference to such an errand is found in an entry in Sanetaka's diary, *Sanetakakōki,* dated the eleventh of the eighth month of 1505, in which Sanetaka judged a collection of Ujichika's

50. See Shimazu, "Rengashi no hanashi," in *Renga no kenkyū,* 300–14.

51. For a review of Sōchō's travels and interactions with provincial warlords, see my "Saiokuken Sōchō and the Linked-Verse Business," *Transactions of the Asiatic Society of Japan,* Fourth Series, vol. 1 (1986): 45–78.

poems and then sent them back via Sōchō.[52] Another reference three years later (the twenty-eighth of the sixth month of 1508) shows Sanetaka sending Ujichika, again through Sōchō's offices, a copy he had made of *Ise monogatari*.[53] Yonehara Masayoshi counts eighteen instances of contact between the Imagawa and Sanetaka, some of them through the agency of Sōchō.[54] But Sanetaka was also Sōchō's own close friend, and *Sanetakakōki* mentions him more than thirty times.[55] He was by no means only a messenger for Ujichika, and when in Suruga he sometimes sent others on personal errands to the Kyoto courtier. Sōchō also helped Ujichika in his collecting of literary works, as he indicates in *Sōchō shuki*: "Over the years I gave various writings to Ujichika as well, either presenting them personally or sending them by messenger" (SS, 135).

Ujichika also made use of his peripatetic *rengashi* as a guide for others—in 1524, for example, Sōchō was obliged to cut short a stay with a local lord in Ise Province to bring a doctor back to Suruga to treat Ujichika (SS, 48). He was also no doubt valuable to Ujichika for the information he absorbed while on his travels about the economic, political, and military conditions of other domains.

On one famous occasion, Sōchō was called on by Ujichika to negotiate with a rival daimyo, Takeda Nobutora (1494–1574), for the lives of an army of one of his generals under siege in Kai Province. Sōchō wrote with understated pride of his accomplishment in *Utsunoyama no ki* soon after the event:

> An army from this province was held within a castle called Katsuyama in Kai Province. The local warlords had had a change of heart and the castle was cut off. On the twenty-second of the first month [of 1517] a local warrior and longtime acquaintance of Ujichika came down and said I must parley with them to bring the matter to a close without incident. Since his order was difficult to refuse, I set out for the provincial capital on the twenty-third. . . . For fifty days I exercised my aged mind in any number of ways in the

52. See Shiba Katsumori, Sanjōnishi Kin'masa, and Korezama Kyōzō, eds., (vols. 1–6); Takahashi Ryuzō, ed., (vols. 7–13), *Sanetakakōki* (Zoku Gunsho Ruijū Kanseikai, 1957–67 [1st printing 1931–38, vols. 1–6]), vol. 4b, 440–41.
53. *Sanetakakōki*, vol. 5a, 62.
54. Yonehara, *Sengoku bushi to bungei no kenkyū*, 857.
55. Ibid.

negotiations between friend and foe, mixing truth and lies. On the second of the third month, two thousand and more Imagawa troops withdrew without a single loss. On my way back, I spent a night at a temple of the Lotus sect called Minobu. At their request:

> The snow and the ice
> vie upon mountains to swell
> the springtime rivers.

yuki kōri / yama ya arasou / haru no mizu

I meant that with the arrival of spring the ice and snow strive to be the first to melt, and then the mountain streams course down. The underlying meaning refers to the peace talks just concluded. (UYK, 400-1)

The encounters with Ujichika that Sōchō records in his diaries are by and large formal in nature. The *renga* sessions Sōchō mentions in which Ujichika took part are nearly all on formal occasions, with Ujichika composing only a single ceremonial verse in his capacity as either host or honored guest. Sōchō also refers to him in his writings with honorifics reserved only for the highest nobility (see p. 139).

Despite that formality, however, the relationship between Sōchō and Ujichika was underscored by personal ties and frequent meetings. Sōchō's diaries do reflect moments of close communion between the two men, as in the section from the *Sōgi shūenki* quoted above where Ujichika took part in poetry and conversation with the other mourners. *Utsunoyama no ki* also recounts a personal moment with the daimyo, when he paid Sōchō the signal honor of coming to visit him in his new hermitage in Mariko, where Ujichika himself had spent his youth:

In the tenth month of the same year [1504/6], Ujichika paid a visit, and we composed a single sheet of twenty-two *renga* verses. The *hokku*:

> How densely grew
> the ivy and maples is clear
> from their fallen leaves!

tsuta kaede / shigerishi shiruki / ochiba kana

It showed very elegant and skillful technique to imply from the fallen leaves how densely they had grown.

> He said afterward that he had been moved by the soaked leaves, which had struggled against the winter rains, then fallen. (UYK, 190)[56]

The episode shows that together with his ceremonial *hokku* and *wakiku,* Ujichika on at least one occasion actually composed an abbreviated verse sequence with Sōchō and later discussed it with him informally. *Utsunoyama no ki* also relates that Sōchō left a prized *shakuhachi* flute with Ujichika when he departed on one of his journeys, which suggests another common interest between the two men. Sōchō's conclusion to *Utsunoyama no ki* not only expresses how he felt when Ujichika returned the prized instrument later on but also indicates that Sōchō meant Ujichika to read the chronicle personally:

> In the spring of the year before last [1515], I left the flute with Ujichika and went to the capital. . . . I sent this account to him, and he must have read it, for a messenger called to say that Ujichika would leave the flute named Old Man with me for a while. He then had it brought over. (UYK, 405)

It was about the time Sōchō composed *Utsunoyama no ki* that Ujichika suffered a stroke (*chūbu*) that left him partially disabled for the rest of his life. This misfortune, plus the advancing age of both men, precluded many of the chances for direct contact that had occurred earlier. Ujichika never again seems to have visited Sōchō's cottage in Mariko.[57] A poem exchange between the two, recorded in *Sōchō shuki,* demonstrates Ujichika's continuing personal regard for Sōchō despite the passage of time:

56. The date of Ujichika's visit could have been 1504 or 1506, depending on that of the building of the cottage in Mariko. See n. 31 above.
57. Sōchō wrote in *Sōchō shuki* in 1527 that Ujichika "suffered his stroke ten years ago," which would date the event roughly to 1517 or 1518. On New Year's Day of 1518, however, Ujichika composed the *hokku* for a hundred-verse sequence for which Saitō Yasumoto made the *wakiku* and Sōchō, the rest (see p. 135). Two days later he wrote the *wakiku* for a *hokku* by Asahina Yasumochi (see p. 132), with Sōchō again composing the last ninety-eight verses. If Ujichika had suffered a stroke before that date, it was clearly not entirely debilitating. Both sequences are extant in manuscript form, in *Shinkei sōzu hyakku ta,* Hiroshima Daigaku, Fukui Bunko.

Ujichika was good enough to send a sprig of blossoming white gentian, with this poem attached:

Unlike all the rest,
how does it happen that this
solitary bough
blossoms with flowers tinted
as if waiting for the snow?

aru ga naka ni / kono hitoeda no / ika ni shite / yuki matsu hana no / iro ni sakuramu

My humble reply:

How could my eye stray
to any of the others?
unlike all the rest,
this sprig is seen as seldom
as the *udonge* blossom.[58]

kazukazu ni / me ya wa utsuramu / aru ga naka ni / mare naru hana wa / udonge ni shite
(SS, 65)

A gathering in honor of Sōchō's longevity held a short time before this exchange shows the esteem in which he was held in the Imagawa domain:

On the last day of the ninth month this autumn [1525], deploring my longevity, I made a poem on the topic of being seventy-eight at the end of the ninth month[59]:

Once again today
the ninth month passes
while this old one remains—
how many more years will turn round
like a spool of flaxen thread?

kyōgoto no / nagatsuki o shi mo / sakidatsuru / oi ni ika naru / shizu no odamaki

58. The *udonge* is a mythical flower that according to Buddhist legend blooms once every three thousand years.
59. Sōchō was seventy-seven by Western count. The Japanese year count (*kazoedoshi*) is retained in this quotation and others from *Sōchō shuki* because of Sōchō's occasional wordplay with numbers.

> Matching this were poems by Ōgimachisanjō Sanemochi, his son Kin'e, Imagawa Ujichika, Sekiguchi Ujikane, Ohara Chikataka, Yui Hōgo, and my disciple Shueki. (SS, 63)

Sōchō and Imagawa Ujiteru

The decrease in the number of Sōchō's meetings with Ujichika was to some extent compensated for by his increasing responsibilities toward the Imagawa heir, Ujiteru. Sōchō recorded a ceremonial interview with him in 1524, then a *renga* session the next year in which the *hokku* was composed by Ujiteru, who at that time was still called by his childhood name Ryūōmaro, which Ujichika had likewise held during his minority (SS, 52). Depending on the formality of the occasion, Sōchō also composed proxy verses (*daisaku*), which were included in linked-verse compositions under Ujiteru's name (SS, 68). Sōchō officiated at the votive *renga* session accompanying Ujiteru's coming-of-age ceremony (*genpuku*) at age twelve late in the eleventh month of 1525 (SS, 67). He subsequently appeared regularly at meetings sponsored by Ujiteru on obligatory poetic occasions such as the Festival of the Weaver Maid (Tanabata) and nights of the full moon. Ujiteru also interacted from an early age with court nobles. In 1525, before his coming-of-age ceremony, he and his father arranged thirty poems each into a poem competition (*uta-awase*) and sent it to Sanetaka for grading, compensating the courtier with two *ryō* in gold for his efforts.[60]

Sōchō's services to Ujiteru were therefore much like those he had performed for his father. And possibly because of the great disparity in age between Sōchō and the young heir, he never depicted their relationship in anything but strictly formal terms in his diaries.

Sōchō's role of literary tutor, however, is much more clearly delineated than in the case of Ujichika. That again is not surprising, given Ujiteru's youth. The passage describing Ujiteru's coming-of-age ceremony shows Sōchō's position as teacher and his respectful attitude toward the heir of the Imagawa:

60. *Sanetakakōki* (1525.9.24), vol. 6b, 30 and (1525.10.2), vol. 6b, 49.

I sent Ujiteru five books of lecture notes and eight sheets of oral teachings on *Kokinshū*. I could not but feel embarrassed by their unreliability, and when Ujiteru has passed his twentieth year and become deeply versed in the way of poetry, he may see for himself that my notes have no value and discard them. If that occurs, I think he ought to consign them to the flames.

> Though it be but slight,
> what I received I bequeath
> to you, my lord,
> that it may be handed down
> and further enrich your house.

> asakeredo / kikishi bakari o / kimi wa kore / waga
> ie no michi ni / tsutaesoenan
> (SS, 67)

Sōchō's guidance appears to have gone beyond the purely literary and to have touched on matters relating to Ujiteru's role as lord of a great warrior household. That is indicated by the postscript Sōchō wrote to *Fuji goran nikki,* in which he described various aspects of Shogun Ashikaga Yorinori's trip to Suruga not covered in the account itself:

> I write with diffidence about details such as these, but do so in order that you may know the great efforts your predecessors made in the past. The lands of your house at that time included only this province. It would not do for you to be unacquainted with earlier matters, and I therefore felt I should relate them here.[61]

Although Ujiteru is not mentioned by name, the date, content, and honorific level of the document indicate it was to have been meant for him.

Sōchō and Ujiteru apparently saw less of each other as the years passed, but they seem to have shared a mutual esteem that lasted until Sōchō's death. However, the moments of familiarity that were noted between Ujichika and his *renga* master are not seen in Sōchō's depictions of his dealings with Ujiteru.

61. *Fuji goran nikki,* in Shirai, *Chūsei no kikō bungaku,* 167–68.

Sōchō and Imagawa Vassals

The level of formality of Sōchō's relationships with Ujichika and Ujiteru becomes clear when compared to his interaction with Yoshitada's widow and certain hereditary Imagawa vassals. Perhaps because of his personal friendship with Yoshitada, Sōchō was one of Lady Kitagawa's "inner circle" and apparently privy to very sensitive confidences. Sōchō recorded a farewell interview he had with her in 1526, just before setting out again for the Kansai:

> On the ninth [of the second month, 1526], after nightfall, I had an audience and celebratory wine with Lady Kitagawa. She favored me with relaxed conversation on various subjects. She was concerned about matters at home and tears wet her sleeves, which saddened me greatly. She said, "I have explained the situation and know you understand—by all means come back from Kyoto." I replied I would do so soon and presently took my leave. Her generous gifts left me at a loss for words. (SS, 75)

Here, Yoshitada's widow shares with Sōchō her concern for the failing health of her son and, by extension, for the stability of the domain. Later, after Ujichika's death, Sōchō cited Lady Kitagawa as one who could give proof of his long service to her husband (see p. 145). Clearly his ties with Yoshitada's wife went far beyond the usual relations between a *renga* master and a daimyo family (see also p. 151, n. 88).

Sōchō's dealings with the many vassals of the Imagawa show great variety.[62] Of them all, he was the closest to the Asahina, vice constables (*shugodai*) of Tōtōmi, and to Saitō Yasumoto, who donated the land for Sōchō's hermitage in Mariko. Many diary entries involving them have a more familiar tone than those involving Ujichika. But other central Imagawa vassals receive little or no treatment in Sōchō's diaries. The Miura, for example, who were house elders (*shukurō*) together with the Asahina, are mentioned in *Sōchō shuki* only once. The Asahina family, particularly Yasumochi,

62. For lists of Imagawa vassals, see Yamamoto Takeshi and Owada Tetsuo, *Sengoku daimyō kashindan jiten, Tōgoku hen,* (Shinjinbutsu Ōraisha, 1981), 319–50, and Ōtsuka Isao, "Sengoku jidai Imagawashi jōsō kashin meibo," in *Suruga no Imagawashi,* vol. 2 (1977), 103–33.

Tokishige, and Yasuyoshi, are included in *Sōchō shuki* nearly as often as the Imagawa themselves, and they played an absolutely central role in Sōchō's Imagawa vassal patronage.[63]

The Asahina were an old family of provincial gentry (*gōzoku*) in Suruga, who entered the service of the first Imagawa constable of that province. They fought on the side of Noritada in the Eikyō Era Discord, and Asahina Yasuhiro, elder brother of Yasumochi and Tokishige, built and then expanded Kakegawa Castle during the incursions into Tōtōmi first by Yoshitada and then by Ujichika. The Asahina also supported the cause of the young Ujichika in his succession battle with Oga Norimitsu, and Yasumochi was a trusted aid to Ujichika both during the latter's youth in Mariko and in his last years after his stroke. *Imagawa kana mokuroku* specifically indicates their privileged position: "Miura Jirōzaemonnojō and Asahina Matatarō [Yasuyoshi?] have fixed places at assembly; the rest may choose their seats accordingly."[64] *Sōchō shuki* states that Yasumochi and Tokishige were Ujichika's milk-brothers (*menotogo*), a relationship traditionally considered one of utmost closeness (SS, 135). Ujichika's grandson Ujizane (1538–1614) was later to fly to Asahina protection at Kakegawa Castle in Tōtōmi after Sunpu was overrun by the armies of Takeda Nobutora's son Shingen (1521–73) in 1568.

Although Sōchō knew Yasuhiro, his close ties to the Asahina family originated with Yasuhiro's younger brothers Yasumochi and Tokishige. Yasumochi's battle exploits figure prominently in Sōchō's Asahina war chronicle, a document not surprisingly biased in favor of Sōchō's patrons. One section reads:

> The watchfires [of the Shiba and their *kokujin* allies] at night were many as the stars in the sky before dawn. Yasumochi easily defeated them and [Shiba Yoshitatsu] retreated. . . . Because of Yasumochi's military success, the province remained peacefully under Imagawa rule. (SS, 10–11)

Sōchō ends the Asahina chronicle by writing:

63. See Matsumoto Masako, "Utsunoyamajō no Asahinashi ni tsuite," in *Suruga no Imagawashi*, vol. 5 (1980), 103–33.
64. Ozawa, "*Imagawa kana mokuroku*," in Imagawashi Kenkyūkai, *Suruga no Imagawashi*, vol. 1, 35.

> Yasumochi served for ten years as advisor to Yasuhiro's son, Yasuyoshi, then relinquished his position and asked leave to go to Suruga, where he lives quietly near the provincial capital. But even so, one hears that he cannot avoid the call to duty.
>
> (SS, 14)

The closeness of the relationship between Yasumochi and Sōchō is vividly suggested in *Sōchō shuki*. Yasumochi seems to have been present at the farewell interview between Sōchō and Lady Kitagawa, and he later personally accompanied him on the first leg of his journey to Kogawa, the home of Hasegawa Motonaga. Motonaga's father, Masanobu, had sheltered Lady Kitagawa and her son during the *Bunmei no naikō* succession dispute (see p. 114). Sōchō records his subsequent parting with Yasumochi as follows:

> . . . as we were about to leave Kogawa, Yasumochi took me by the sleeve and recited this poem:
>
> Now that we must part,
> who can I look to in
> the days ahead
> for the guiding counsel
> that a loving parent gives?
>
> tachiwakare / ima yori nochi wa / tarachine no / oya no isame to / tare o omowan
>
> My reply:
>
> While reflecting with
> esteem upon the long lives
> of your grandfather,
> your father, and then yourself,
> I am struck by my own age.
> (SS, 76)
>
> ōji chichi / kimi made oi ga / nagaiki o / awaremu ni tsukete / odorokarenuru

Moreover, part of the section near the end of *Sōchō shuki* where Sōchō outlines his contributions to the Imagawa is directly addressed to Yasumochi in the form of a letter, which indicates that he was one of Sōchō's most influential supporters.

Sōchō also enjoyed a close personal relationship with Yasumochi's younger brother Tokishige, who is afforded a place of honor in the Asahina chronicle for defending Kakegawa Castle in the absence of Yasumochi (SS, 11). One of the entries in *Sōchō shuki* most revealing of Sōchō's character and personality describes a meeting where, in Sōchō's words, "Tokishige came to visit, and we had a pleasant conversation by the hearth about year-end frustrations, repayment of loans, allotments of rice stipends, and the lack of enough of anything" (SS, 70). Part of that section will be examined here in more detail further on in another context.

To Yasuyoshi, the young heir whom Yasumochi served as advisor, Sōchō appears to have acted more as a tutor than as a personal friend, much as was the case with Ujiteru. That is again understandable, given the disparity in their ages. One scholar of Sōchō has suggested that the first of the two books of *Sōchō shuki* was written to instruct the young Asahina heir in the history of his house and the deportment of a warrior.[65] Although it seems unlikely in view of the variety of the journal that the whole of Book One was written with a single recipient in mind, it is possible that Sōchō presented a copy of the work to the Asahina and that Yasuyoshi read it. The notion correlates well with the fact that another of the many functions of a *renga* master was to write travel diaries and other diverting and instructive material for patrons.

Yasumochi and Tokishige are thus depicted in Sōchō's diaries in terms of greater familiarity than is their overlord, Ujichika. That is underscored by Sōchō's references to economic support from them. He mentions being sent two *ryō* in gold from Yasumochi and Tokishige near the end of 1526 (SS, 108), and he receives a short-sleeved robe (*kosode*) from Tokishige a year later (SS, 142–43). There are no explicit references to money or valuables received directly from Ujichika.

In return, Sōchō provided the Asahina with many of the same services he performed for the Imagawa, particularly as *renga* master and chronicler. He also executed votive *renga* for them, such as a sequence of three hundred verses he composed alone on the death of Asahina Yasaburō in 1510, and a celebratory *hokku* on the completion in 1516 of a Hachiman shrine at their Kakegawa Castle (SS, 11).[66] As vice constables of Tōtōmi, the Asahina were committed to the cultural

65. Iwashita Noriyuki, "*Sōchō shuki* no chosaku ito ni tsuite," *Kokubungaku kenkyū* 65 (June 1978): 19–20.

66. Yonehara, *Sengoku bushi to bungei no kenkyū*, 881.

as well as military improvement of Kakegawa Castle and the town surrounding it, and as Sunpu became more and more a provincial Kyoto, Kakegawa developed in turn as a provincial Sunpu and cultural satellite of the Imagawa capital. And despite their absolute loyalty to their overlord, they too devoted themselves to cultural pursuits, not only, one may infer, to symbolize by extension the grandeur of the Imagawa but to emphasize their own subsidiary authority within their sphere of influence.

Like Ujichika, Yasuyoshi allied himself to the court aristocracy by marriage to the granddaughter of Nakamikado Nobutane, a union effected partly through Jukei.[67] The marriage also bound him more closely to his Imagawa overlords, of course. Poetic gatherings sponsored by the Asahina were on a higher level of sophistication than those of many daimyo houses—Sōchō even gives the details of a linked-verse session in Chinese and Japanese sponsored by Tokishige (SS, 68). Such *wakan renku* required a high level of scholarship, one seldom attained by warrior poets. Sōchō was thus as important to Asahina cultural aspirations as they were to his political and financial support. But though Sōchō seems to have enjoyed even greater familiarity with Yasumochi and Tokishige than with Ujichika himself, those relationships probably originated through mutual Imagawa ties, and they were certainly reinforced by those ties subsequently.

The third main source of Sōchō's support in the Suruga domain was Saitō Yasumoto, lord of Mariko Castle. It will be recalled that it was Yasumoto who provided Sōchō with his Brushwood Cottage in Mariko. As he did with the Asahina, Sōchō composed *renga* with Yasumoto, and the daimyo of course countenanced the relationship—a hundred-verse sequence involving Yasumoto, Ujichika, and Sōchō survives from New Year's Day, 1518.[68] Sōchō and Yasumoto also frequently interacted on a direct, personal basis without Imagawa involvement. The proximity of Yasumoto to Sōchō's Brushwood Cottage made it particularly easy for him to see Sōchō and to profit from his poetic guidance. Sōchō's diary of 1509, *Azumaji no tsuto,* begins, in fact, with a *renga* session at Yasumoto's, but without Ujichika:

67. Hori Akira, "Imagawashi jūshin no kon'in kankei," in *Suruga no Imagawashi,* vol. 6, 117–18.
68. See n. 57.

I had been meaning to set out for Shirakawa Gate "in the springtime haze," but year after year passed.[69] Finally I decided I must in any event go this autumn and set the date for the sixteenth of the seventh month, sixth year of Eishō [1509].

On that day, Saitō Kaganokami Yasumoto, who resides next to my thatched cottage, arranged a session for the composition of a single sheet of linked verse. Unable to refuse, I composed this *hokku*:

> See them in the wind—
> kudzu leaves that show I will
> soon be coming home!

kaze ni miyo / ima kaerikon / kuzuha kana

I was simply recalling here the old poem that goes, "... growing by our parting path."[70] At the time, I was in the mountain village of Mariko.[71]

---

69. Sōchō makes reference to a poem by Nōin (*Goshūishū,* vol. 9, 518):

Composed at Shirakawa Gate while on a trip to Michinoku:

> Though I set out from
> the imperial city
> in the springtime haze,
> now the wind of autumn blows
> at Shirakawa Gate.

miyako o ba / kasumi to tomo ni / tachishikado /
akikaze zo fuku / shirakawa no seki

Sōkyū in *Miyako no tsuto* and Sōgi in *Shirakawa kikō* likewise refer to the poem.

70. Sōchō also quotes this *hokku* in his first collection of verses, *Kabekusa,* and, in slightly different form, in *Utsunoyama no ki.* The *honka* is the following (*Shūishū,* vol. 6, 306, anon.):

> You must not forget
> that when the autumn wind blows
> through the kudzu leaves
> growing by our parting path
> I will soon be coming home.

wasuru na yo / wakareji ni ouru / kuzu no ha no /
akikaze fukeba / ima kaerikon

The autumn wind blowing through the kudzu leaves reveals their white undersides to elegant effect. Kudzu is thus traditionally associated with the verb *kaeru,* "to turn over," and to its homonym, "to return home."

71. *Azumaji no tsuto,* in *Gunsho ruijū,* vol. 18, 770.

For Yasumoto, proximity fostered particularly close ties to Sōchō, but also meant a greater burden of responsibility. Sōchō explicitly refers to him in *Utsunoyama no ki* as "the donor of my thatched cottage" (*sōan no danna*; UYK, 402) and duns him outright in a humorous and familiar way for daily necessities:

> I wrote to the donor of my thatched cottage, Yasumoto, requesting various things for the end of the year, and added:
>
> Two bags of charcoal,
> twenty bundles of firewood,
> radishes, burdock,
> two straw-wrapped packets of food—
> I am awaiting your reply!
>
> sumi futako / takigi nijippa / tsuto futatsu / daikon gobō / kaeshi o zo matsu
>
> (UYK, 402)

Sōchō subsequently sends a poem of thanks, in an equally light vein:

> In my thatched cottage,
> so much evidence, good sir,
> of your kind regard—
> I find myself at year end
> full of both goods and thanks!
>
> kusa no iori / kazukazu kimi ga / kokorozashi / okidokoro naki / toshi no kure kana
>
> (UYK, 402)

Sōchō even depended on Yasumoto to be the temporary guardian for his son, Jōha (UYK, 404). While Lady Kitagawa and Asahina Yasumochi and Tokishige may have been more politically influential members of the Imagawa house, Yasumoto certainly bore much of the burden of Sōchō's support. Sōchō in turn was obligated to compose *renga* with Yasumoto even when anxious to set out on his trip to Shirakawa; his phrase "unable to refuse" (*ji shigatakute*) is not only an expression of humble diffidence but a recognition of obligation. The same was of course true for the Asahina—Sōchō uses the word "unavoidable" (*sarigataki ni yori*) in reference to a thousand-link sequence with Yasumochi and others in 1526 (SS, 76).

A large number of other Imagawa vassals also figure in *Sōchō shuki,* some limited to one appearance and others taking regular part in literary activities with Sōchō. His interaction with those other vassals, like that with the Asahina and Yasumoto, was based on personal ties established with individuals, not to all vassals in a monolithic fashion. Sōchō's contact with members of the Okitsu family, for example, continued over a long period and was marked by particular rapport. In their fief were located Kiyomi Strand and Seikenji, to which Sōchō as a young man had invited Sōgi and Shōkō. On his later visits to Okitsu lands, Sōchō was called on for the nearly inevitable *renga* sessions, and he also actively tutored family members in the literary arts. One of the two parts of his well-known *Sōchō renga jichū* ("Personal Commentary on Verses by Sōchō," 1517) was addressed to Okitsu Masanobu.[72] A passage in *Sōchō shuki* relating to Masanobu's heir Hikokurō (Chikahisa) is particularly valuable for the degree of closeness it shows between Sōchō and an Imagawa retainer, and also for the contrast it presents with Sōchō's attitude toward Imagawa Ujichika and Ujiteru. The lines immediately follow those in which Sōchō was honored with *waka* congratulating him on his longevity by Ujichika and other elevated men of the domain (see pp. 128–29):

> Okitsu Hikokurō requested the poem strips. I sent them, thinking they would make good models for poetic composition. They were so elegant that I was moved to add another:
>
> Today autumn passes—
> how many more ninth months are
> left for this old one?
> Before the end more will turn round,
> like a spool of flaxen thread.
>
> kyō ni kurete / iku aki oi no / nagatsuki ya / yuku sue mo nao / shizu no odamaki
>
> At the beginning of winter, Hikokurō sent me a goose. I included this in my reply to his appended letter:
>
> It is the tenth month,
> and I behold the wild goose,
> its wings entwined,
> whose call was the first one that
> I heard in the autumn wind.

72. *Sōchō renga jichū,* in vol. 18 of Shiba Katsumori and Yamagishi Tokuhei, eds., *Katsuranomiyabon sōsho* (Yōtokusha, 1968), 95–183.

oto ni nomi / hatsukarigane no / akikaze no /
tsubasa o kawasu / kannazuki kana
(SS, 64–65)

Thereafter follows the passage in which Ujichika sends Sōchō the poem with a sprig of gentian (see p. 128). In comparison to the diffidence of his remarks on presenting *Kokinshū* documents to Ujiteru, the straightforward and unapologetic nature of Sōchō's correspondence with Hikokurō is immediately apparent. And Sōchō addresses Hikokurō as an equal, with no honorifics (*kari o hitotsu fumi ni soete motekitaru. Sono henji ni . . .*). The succeeding passage on Ujichika's letter and gentian sprig, by contrast, uses high honorifics (*rindō no shiroku sakeru hitoeda o miserarehaberu ni soeraretamau uta . . . onkaeshi*). The difference in Sōchō's perception of his relation to an Imagawa vassal as opposed to the daimyo himself is obvious.

The Linked-Verse Profession

Having considered the kinds and nature of Sōchō's ties to the Imagawa family and their close retainers, we should now examine the tangible rewards Sōchō received for his services to those various clients. At the outset it must be admitted that it is impossible to determine Sōchō's annual income. Sōchō's diaries were written with more artistic intent than the *kanbun* diaries of courtiers, and money was not a "literary" topic. Nevertheless, his writings do supply many hints—far more than other travel diaries of the period—as to the size and nature of his livelihood. He had essentially two sources of support—the Imagawa and their vassals on the one hand and various daimyo and gentry of select non-Imagawa domains on the other. His frequent travels were partly made with the desire to see poetic places, acquire fresh artistic inspiration, visit temples (often related to Ikkyū), and renew acquaintances with old friends, but also to call on the wealthy and increase his income by directing *renga* sessions and providing oral and written instruction on poetry and the classics. The focus here is on Sōchō's relationship with the Imagawa, but his very considerable support from other sources must not be forgotten. One quotation by Sōchō relating to money received from Mizuno Chikamori of Mikawa Province gives a vivid picture of the economic importance of such sources:

> Five hundred *hiki* as a gift. Last year too when I left for Kyoto, I received one thousand *hiki* as a going-away present. Totaling these and other favors received from him to date, I find they reach ten thousand *hiki*. Overwhelming! Just overwhelming! (SS, 124–25).[73]

The passage also indicates that Sōchō probably retained records of the sources and amounts of his revenue.

By contrast, Sōchō only once mentions money received from any of the three Imagawa daimyo themselves, and that was in the form of a gift from Ujiteru specifically in thanks for funeral presents brought in memory of Ujichika (SS, 135). Sōchō does, however, record gifts received from Lady Kitagawa, money and clothing from Asahina Yasumochi and Tokishige, and provisions from Saitō Yasumoto. The postscript of *Imagawa kafu* as well says that Sōchō rewrote the work into *kana* (actually *wakankonkōbun,* a combination of *kana* and Chinese characters) for compensation in "rice money" (*komedai*).[74] Kidō Saizō suspects Sōchō received a "fixed income" from the Imagawa, but he does not provide any evidence.[75] The assumption is a likely one, however, in light of the existence of a residence in Sunpu and the relatively comfortable standard of living depicted in the diaries. Sōchō also had the wherewithal to donate, by his own reckoning, thirty thousand *hiki* to Daitokuji over the course of his life (partly by selling a prized copy of *Genji monogatari*; SS, 62). He also owned valuable artwork, such as a Yuan-period painting of one of the views of the Xiao and Xiang rivers.[76]

Nevertheless, *Sōchō shuki* and *Sōchō nikki* include a number of references to neediness, most notably in part of a *chōka* ("long poem") he writes on hermitage (*sōan*) life:

> But though my cottage
> offers me so rich a choice

73. Sōchō wrote *Wakurabachū,* a commentary on Sōgi's second personal poetry collection, *Wakuraba,* at Chikamori's request in 1520 and visited him on each of the four trips between Suruga and the Kansai covered in *Sōchō shuki*. On Chikamori and the Mizuno house, see Suzuki Mitsuyasu, "Mikawa ni okeru Sōchō oboegaki," *Matsumura Hiroshi Kyōju taikan kinen kokugo kokubungaku ronshū* (1973), 318–21.
74. *Imagawa kafu,* 159–60.
75. Kidō, "Sengoku shoki," 177.
76. By Yu Jian. See Yamanoue Sōji, *Chaki meibutsushū, Zoku gunsho ruijū,* vol 19b, 473–74.

of changing vistas,
thoughts that come to mind the most
are of food and funds
and cloudy cups of sake
I sip so seldom—
to be sure, I have people
coming and going
day after day without fail
to pay me visits,
but they bring nothing with them,
naught I have to give,
so sated just in spirit
I can only ask,
"Will you take at least some tea?"
meager as that is—

toridori ni / miru wa kotonaru / yado nagara / omou koto to wa / meshi oashi / nigori kukon mo / maremare ni / sasuga ni hito no / ideiri wa / tayuru hi mo naku / miekuredo / nani motekoneba / motenasazu / mune nomi sumite / tsurezure to / oncha o dani to / iu bakari
(SS, 53)

Much of this is perhaps literary pose, and it is in any case not good business to imply to one's patron that one needs no more support. In his last years his financial situation seems to have eroded somewhat, but it is unlikely he was ever truly in want. An entry in *Sōchō shuki* for 1527, for example, describes new construction at his Mariko cottage (SS, 131–32).

In addition to Sōchō's material assistance from the Imagawa—whatever its amount and nature—his relationship with them had additional benefits. One of those was the security, so necessary in those violent times, that Imagawa patronage provided. With Imagawa support also came entree into the Imagawa vassal network in Suruga and Tōtōmi, as well as a natural connection to other literary figures in the Imagawa capital. And it is likely he had at least some access to the Imagawa library, one of the finest among daimyo households.

But this close affiliation also hindered Sōchō's freedom in some ways. Orders from Ujichika were unconditional. Sōchō's record of his negotiations with Takeda Nobutora in 1517 relates that Ujichika's "command was difficult to refuse" (*kimei somukigatakute*; UYK, 400), and his account of cutting short his stay with a local warlord in Ise Province to escort the doctor back to Suruga for Ujichika includes the word "unavoidable" (*sarigatakute*; SS, 47). His relationship with the Imagawa also meant obligatory *renga* sessions on formal occasions. And Sōchō's well-known connection with them may have prevented him from widening his circle of acquaintances to include daimyo and other warriors hostile to their house. In addition, Sōchō's personal contact and support from Ujichika and Ujiteru left him vulnerable to criticism from their detractors within the Imagawa camp. Let us turn now to the nature and circumstances behind this last matter, which seems to have significantly altered the quality of Sōchō's life in Suruga in his last years.

Sōchō in Old Age, Sunpu in Transition

Ujichika died in the sixth month of 1526 after having suffered for nearly a decade with palsy. His funeral was of proportions befitting his grandeur—it is written that eight hundred retainers and seven thousand monks participated.[77] In his last years he had been aided in matters of government by his highest vassals and also by his wife Jukei. Ujiteru succeeded to the position of daimyo, but though he had undergone the coming-of-age ceremony he was still little more than a child. Jukei therefore acted as his advisor, and documents bearing her seal remain from her nearly two-year de facto regency and thereafter as well.

Sōchō was staying at Shūon'an, Ikkyū's old hermitage in Takigi in Yamashiro Province, when Ujichika died, and he received notice of Ujichika's death a month after it had occurred. He did not, however, go immediately back to Sunpu and pay his respects, nor, oddly enough, did he record anything about the event in his diary until the following entry, written in retrospect fully one year later:

> Aside from Ujichika, Lords Bōshū and Zushū have passed away as well—how is it I too did not awake from this dream in the past year?
>
> A count of my years
> shows me to have been older
> than the others
> who have gone before me.
> And I can do nothing.

77. *Imagawa Ujichikakō sōki,* in Owada, *Shizuokashi shi,* 1087.

kazoureba / ware taga tame mo / kono kami no /
shiniokurekinu / kore ika ni semu

(SS, 128)

From a later diary section, though, we know that Sōchō observed the requisite funeral proprieties privately in Takigi and also in the next months set about acquiring poetic offerings to be presented at Sunpu when he did return.

That winter, war broke out in the environs of the capital between the forces of Yanagimoto Kataharu and those of Shogun Ashikaga Yoshiharu (1511–50) and his ally Hosokawa Takakuni (1484–1531), and for that reason Sōchō subsequently moved to another temple related to Ikkyū, Shōrinji in Yashima, east of Lake Biwa. His diary suggests his disquiet at the time:

Though across the lake, I still heard news of the disruption in the capital:

Even here, even here,
those most distressing tidings
do not cease to come
wind-borne from the capital
across the white-capped billows.

koko mo koko mo / mimi yasukaranu / shiranami
no / miyako no kaze no / tsute shi taeneba

(SS, 102)

Sōchō finally departed for Sunpu in the third month of the next year, 1527, and arrived at the beginning of summer with a number of others, including his disciple Tani Sōboku (?–1545).

When he reached the Imagawa capital, however, Sōchō seems to have been met with hostility in some quarters. The traditional explanation for that is given in the old edition of the history of Shizuoka City (*Shizuokashi shi*), published in 1931: "Criticism of Sōchō mounted in Sunpu when he did not immediately return after receiving news of Ujichika's death."[78] Recently, however, in an article entitled "Sōchō—Misunderstood in the Shōwa Era," Nakagawa Yoshio has challenged that assumption and argued instead that the old theory was the result of a misreading of Sōchō's elliptical and

78. Tsuge Kiyoshi et al., *Shizuokashi shi* (Shizuoka City: Shizuoka Shiyakusho, 1931), 380.

occasionally ambiguous prose.[79] He holds that there was no reason for criticism since Sōchō observed the funeral proprieties and returned with splendid gifts for Ujichika's memory and for the young heir, which were gratefully accepted. The messenger informing Sōchō of Ujichika's death may not even have left Sunpu until after the funeral was over. Nakagawa reasons that the criticism Sōchō speaks of after his return to Suruga was directed not at him but instead at the late daimyo and his son.

Nakagawa also points out that the transfer of power was not entirely free of contention and that the Kogawa residence of Hasegawa Motonaga, whose father Masanobu had protected Ujichika during his minority, was razed (see p. 114).[80] Perhaps relatives of Oga Norimitsu, the man that Ujichika had deposed with Hōjō Sōun's help four decades earlier, were making another bid for power. It will be recalled that Sōchō had visited Motonaga in the previous year in the company of Yasumochi (see p. 133). Sōchō knew, from his personal experiences exactly a half-century before, of the potential for instability after a daimyo's death, and he may have postponed his departure from the Kansai to see what would happen. He wrote in his diary for the eleventh month of that year of a visit from Suruga by a member of the Asahina family, and added, "All well in Suruga and Tōtōmi. That above all is a cause for rejoicing" (SS, 108). The remark may refer to Takeda Nobutora's abortive incursion into Suruga immediately after Ujichika's death, or to unrest within the house, but in either case the fact that all was now well may have contributed to Sōchō's decision to return.[81]

But a reexamination of Sōchō's own detailed account of his return to Suruga, the criticism he encountered, and the history of his service to the family (which was in part quoted earlier in this study)

79. Nakagawa Yoshio, "Sōchō wa Shōwaki ni gokai sareta," in Owada, *Shizuokashi shi,* 1319–41.
80. Tsurusaki Hirō also makes reference to an "anti-Ujichika faction" in his "Araara muge no niwazuki sōrō kana: Rengashi Sōchō no bannen," *Tezukayama Gakuin Tanki Daigaku kenkyū nenpō* 26 (1978): 14.
81. Nobutora invaded Suruga the month after Ujichika died. In Suntō District, eastern Suruga, he defeated an ally of the Imagawa, Hōjō Ujitsuna (1486–1541), son of Hōjō Sōun and first cousin of Ujichika. But Nobutora appears to have subsequently retired without pursuing his advantage (see *Myōhōjiki,* in Shimizu Shigeo and Hattori Harunori, eds., *Takeda shiryōshū,* vol. 13 of *Dai ni ki sengoku shiryō sōsho* [Jinbutsu Ōraisha, 1966–17], 36).

suggests that there are elements of truth in both the old and the new theories. Sōchō's account is at least in part a letter to Asahina Yasumochi, which indicates that in addition to providing material assistance, Yasumochi was a main source of spiritual support. Sōchō begins by giving the date on which he heard of Ujichika's death, then writes:

> I should have gone to pay my last respects on hearing of Ujichika's death, but I was already in my seventy-ninth year and thought it was to be my last, so I had requested leave to prepare for my end at Daitokuji or Takigi. (SS, 135)

Sōchō here refers to a prophesy he mentions earlier (SS, 105) that he was to die in his seventy-ninth year (by the Japanese count). It was this sentence that gave rise to the supposition that Sōchō was criticized for not returning sooner to Suruga.

Next, Sōchō explains in detail the offerings he made for Ujichika's repose and his request of Sanetaka "to arrange for each of the various courtly houses to present a poem on a book of the *Lotus Sutra* as a prayer for the repose of the deceased" (SS, 135). He also recounts his trips to Yashima and Suruga, and his pleasure at the reception of the sutra poems ("The reading of the sutra poems was particularly appreciated" [SS, 135]).

Sōchō then provides the brief history of his relationship with the Imagawa we have mentioned earlier:

> I also brought a copy of *Kokinshū,* personally completed last year by Lord Sanetaka, which I had requested eight or nine years previously. I had already presented to Ujiteru as a little memento three books and a box of loose papers on the secret traditions of that collection when I left for the capital last year. They were given to me by Sōgi. Over the years I gave various writings to Ujichika as well, either presenting them personally or sending them by messenger.
>
> Though I was in no special service to Lord Yoshitada, I was close to him day and night for years. No one knows that now, though Lady Kitagawa may remember it. She said as much when she summoned me into her presence—when was it? At that time Asahina Yasumochi was also in respectful attendance on her.[82]

82. This may be the interview mentioned on p. 131 (SS, 75).

When Ujichika was a child, I took my leave to spend time at Daitokuji. He showed me great consideration. For twenty years I came and went from the capital and enjoyed his special favor. Everyone must know that. Moreover, from time to time I was of service to him.

Then when I returned in the fourth month of this year, I learned of events in the province and saw things for myself. Nothing seemed real. Not a year has passed since Ujichika's death. I can only wonder in amazement how all could have changed so. (SS, 135–36)

After this account, Sōchō quotes his letter to Yasumochi on the condition in which he found the domain on his return. He begins with a poem of lament (*jukkai*):

Though I told myself
if it must be, it must be,
my eyes and ears are
surfeited in sight and sound
with many too many mouths.[83]

sa mo araba / are to omoedo / me ni mimi ni / kikite mo mite mo / amaru kuchi zo yo

I am saddened by the falsehood I encounter everywhere.[84] I have heard nothing but doubts voiced about judgments and policies made after Ujichika suffered his stroke ten years ago. Ujiteru, they continue, is a boy not yet twenty, unstable and willful with those in his service. When I returned to this domain, I heard nothing but slander, groundless rumor, and outrageous insolence, some directed even at me. Were it meant for me alone I would not be bothered. It may seem that I am defending them to all and sundry, but I wanted at the very least to plead their case and

83. This *waka* appears in four different forms in the *Gunsho ruijū* text of *Sōchō shuki* (18:323), the *Zoku gunsho ruijū* text of *Sōchō nikki* (18:1259) and the Iwanami Bunko texts of *Sōchō shuki* (p. 136) and *Sōchō nikki* (in Shimazu Tadao, ed., *Sōchō nikki* [Iwanami Bunko, 1975], 154). All future references to *Sōchō nikki* will be indicated in the text as SN; the numbers that follow SN refer to page. The last is the clearest and most regular metrically, and I have accordingly substituted it for the garbled and irregular Iwanami Bunko versions.

84. I have emended *kako* ("past") in the Iwanami Bunko manuscript to *kagen* ("falsehood") on the basis of the *Gunsho ruijū* text (p. 323).

> gave free rein to my brush. But I can do nothing about the ever-present rumors, protest them though I will. Anyone can imagine my vexation. I pressed for an investigation several times, but it had no effect. Moreover, the slanderers came out in the open. In the end nothing could be done, and so I prepared to meet my end at my Brushwood Cottage in Mariko. But Mariko is only just across the river from Tegoshi, and people are always coming and going. What painful matters for these aged ears! (SS, 136–37)

Sōchō's statement makes it clear that Ujichika's death was indeed accompanied by forces of unrest in the domain. He does not mention divisive elements in his diary during Ujichika's lifetime, but when he returns from the Kansai he wonders "in amazement how all could have changed so." His subsequent remarks on Ujichika and Ujiteru show that Nakagawa is correct in saying that the criticism Sōchō encounters is directed at the *ancien régime* and the young successor.

But it is equally plain that the old theory is in part correct too, insofar as criticism was leveled at Sōchō as well. Sōchō clearly writes that some of the "slander, groundless rumor, and outrageous insolence" was "directed even at me" (*warera tei made*). He also mentions two other difficulties he encountered after returning to Sunpu that may indicate antagonism toward him.

The first involved a letter of introduction he sent on behalf of his disciple Sōboku and Sōboku's companions to Seikenji at Kiyomi Strand (the same *uta-makura* to which he had invited Sōgi and Shōkō over half a century before [see pp. 111–13]), which had little effect:

> Some visitors said they wanted to see the site of the old Kiyomi Gate, and I gave them a letter of introduction to take with them to Seikenji. When they returned, they said nothing about the trip to me, so I appended this poem to my answer to a letter from Okitsu Hikokurō:
>
> If they would be so,
> I will try calling myself
> something different;
> was it the name "Sōchō"
> that made them unresponsive?
>
> iza saraba / waga na o kaete / yobite mimu / sōchō yue ya / tsurenakaruramu
>
> (SS, 128)

The second difficulty occurred on the occasion of the first anniversary of Ujichika's death. Sōchō composed poems for the repose of the deceased, but no one made a clean copy for him:

> Sixth month, twenty-third day [of 1527]—first anniversary of the death of Imagawa Ujichika. I composed a solo hundred-verse sequence beginning each verse with a syllable from the first five syllables of twenty of his poems:
>
> The breeze from this fan,
> a keepsake, makes him even
> harder to forget.
>
> kaze wa nao / wasuregatami no / ōgi kana
>
> I tried to order a fair copy but could find no one to do it for me. There was nothing for it but to entrust the work to my own aged brush:
>
> These remnants from
> this eighty-year-old's brush,
> which in any case
> never moved but haltingly,
> will serve as a parting prayer.
>
> sarade dani / yukitodokōru / mizukuki no / yasoji no ato mo / tamuke to zo omou
>
> (SS, 129)

Sōchō's diary is free of such episodes prior to his return from Yashima after Ujichika's death, which may indicate a link between these two rebuffs and the "outrageous insolence" Sōchō mentions.

We may never know the sources or reasons for the criticism of Sōchō. The forces who burned the Kogawa residence may have been involved, but the connection needs to be investigated further. Sōchō may also have in fact been vilified for not hurrying back, but again there is no proof. It is true, however, that Sōchō was still deploring criticism from some quarter even four years later, as shown in an entry in *Sōchō nikki* for 1530, where he requotes his "Though I told myself" (*sa mo araba*) poem of 1527 (SN, 154; see p. 146).

The firm evidence that remains indicates that Ujichika and Ujiteru were criticized, as was Sōchō, and that Sōchō defended himself to Yasumochi by reiterating his service to three generations of Imagawa leaders. Sōchō's relationship with the three Imagawa daimyo laid him open to criticism from some quarters, and at the same time exculpated him in the eyes of those, like Yasumochi, who were loyal to the old order. The affair demonstrates the fact that Sōchō's healthy relationship with the Imagawa house was guaranteed through the personal goodwill of a strong daimyo. Sōchō's diaries indicate that his ties with the young Ujiteru do not appear to have been as close as those with Ujichika, and although the vassals with whom Sōchō had personal bonds continued to support him, his life in Suruga became less secure.

Sōchō nevertheless continued in the service of Ujiteru, who began issuing documents under his own name in 1528. Had there been an actual break between Ujiteru and Sōchō, his ties to even his closest contacts among the Imagawa vassals would have been jeopardized. Sōchō continued to compose verses at formal *renga* sessions at Ujiteru's residence, and in one case he reminded the young daimyo of the history of his house:

> The Festival of the Weaver Maid arrived. There was a *waka* series at Ujiteru's residence. He had meant to do it without prearranged topics, but I said that because in an earlier day Imagawa Sadayo [Ryōshun] and Norimasa had been the disciples of Reizei Tamehide and Tamemasa, there was no need to be diffident, and so we had a session based on thirty topics chosen by Ujiteru. (SN, 148)

Iwashita Noriyuki has made the suggestion that Sōchō presented the second book of *Sōchō shuki* to Ujiteru and the Imagawa house in response to the criticism circulating at the time.[85] Iwashita gives the long protest letter quoted here earlier in support of his view and cites the more formal tone of the second book in corroboration. As was mentioned with regard to his suggestion that Book One was meant for Asahina Yasuyoshi, it seems unlikely that Sōchō had a single recipient in mind during the entire time he wrote Book Two, but it is very possible that he intended to present the Imagawa with a copy of the finished product to reinforce his position in the domain.

Even after Ujichika's death, Sōchō still enjoyed the favor of his earlier patrons. He continued to receive gifts and poems from Tokishige, wrote to Yasumochi, and maintained his ties with Lady Kitagawa. The Okitsu apparently still helped him as well, for the letter of protest appears to have been written while he was in their fief. The courtier Ōgimachisanjō Kin'e, Lady Kitagawa's grandson,

85. Iwashita, "*Sōchō shuki* no chosaku ito," 23.

visited him, as did Nakamikado Nobutane's son Nobuhide. He was also still called on to work in his old capacity as chronicler, being commissioned to rewrite *Imagawa kafu.* But there is no disguising the increasing loneliness of Sōchō's last years, as one by one his old supporters died, leaving him more and more isolated in a domain with active detractors. Okitsu Moritsuna died in 1528; Lady Kitagawa in 1529; and Kin'e's wife, his father Sanemochi, and Tō Sojun in 1530. With the loss of those old acquaintances there was no doubt a corresponding loss of revenue for Sōchō in the form of gifts. Of his increasing loneliness, Sōchō writes in *Sōchō nikki*:

> The days are tedious in my mountain cottage during the long rains. Here I have none for friends save the snails:
>
> In the summer rains
> the snails that come dancing out
> from among the drops
> that spill from off of the rocks
> are the only ones who call.
>
> samidare wa / iwa no shizuku no / maiizuru /
> katatsuburi o zo / tou hito ni suru
> (SN, 147)

Nor could he travel as he once did. His physical condition seems to have deteriorated along with the political climate, limiting him to relatively short excursions to Atami and Odawara. Sōchō wrote: "Recently I have been suffering cruelly from the flux, and to make matters worse, I have been having numbness of the legs—I crawl along like a dog crushed by a cart, completely unfit for travel" (SS, 137). His loss of mobility cut him off from the provincial gentry who were his second major source of income. The number of *renga* verses in *Sōchō nikki,* his last diary, is greatly exceeded by *uta,* which again suggests a decline in his professional activities.[86]

Neither does he seem to have established a strong personal relationship with Ujichika's wife, Jukei, whose name never once appears in his writings. Such a connection might have intensified his relationship with Ujiteru, given Jukei's strong influence on her young son's affairs. Her de facto rule of the domain continued from the time

86. There are eighty-six *waka* in *Sōchō nikki,* nearly all by Sōchō himself, and only eight of Sōchō's *renga* verses, excluding a final fifty-verse section taken from one of his thousand-verse solo sequences.

of Ujichika's death in 1526 until Ujiteru assumed control in 1528, a period covering three quarters of the second book of *Sōchō shuki.*[87] We know from other sources that she took an interest in literature (she ordered a commentary on *Genji monogatari* from Sanetaka), and the lack of references to her in Sōchō's account would seem to imply that she looked to others for advice on literary matters. In light of Sōchō's deep friendship with her father, Nakamikado Nobutane, her absence from Sōchō's diaries seems even more significant. It may of course be that the criticism of Ujichika and Ujiteru that Sōchō mentions was also directed at Ujiteru's de facto regent, Jukei, and that Sōchō's recital in his journal of his loyalty to the old order was meant for her eyes as well.[88]

87. See Kubota Masaki, "Imagawa Ujichika kōshitsu Jukeini hakkyū no monjo ni tsuite," *Komazawa shigaku* 24 (1977): 135–48 and "Imagawa Ujiteru to sono monjo," *Komazawa Daigaku Daigakuin shigaku ronshū* 8 (1978): 37–46.
88. One popularized and at times fictional account of Sōchō's life by Saitō Sakae sees Sōchō's relationship with Lady Kitagawa and the nun Jukei as central to the events of his last years. Saitō asserts that Sōchō was sexually involved with Imagawa Yoshitada and that he became so with Lady Kitagawa as well for a short time after Yoshitada's death in battle in 1476. Saitō suggests that the young Sōchō left for the Kansai thereafter because of the danger such an affair constituted, but that Lady Kitagawa nevertheless remained the focus of his spiritual ties to the Imagawa house for the rest of his life. Jukei, Saitō theorizes, detested her mother-in-law and, by obvious extension, Sōchō, and as Ujichika's own power waned in the years after his stroke, the security of his mother and Sōchō eroded accordingly. Sōchō's decision to leave Suruga in 1526, Saitō believes, was due to the realization that his position would be untenable after the death of his protector, then in physical decline. Lady Kitagawa anticipated the same would be true in her own case, and their mutual misgivings about the future lay at the heart of their meeting on the eve of Sōchō's departure and her request that he hurry back to Suruga (SS, 75–76). When Ujichika died, concludes Saitō, Jukei had no further need to hide her animosity, and Sōchō postponed his departure from Takigi accordingly, finally returning to Suruga in 1527 only to honor his promise to Lady Kitagawa to do so. Much of Saitō's account is complete fabrication, and many points, such as the assumption that it was Jukei herself who was at the center of the anti-Ujichika faction and the source of the slander against Sōchō, are unsubstantiated. The assertion that Lady Kitagawa and Sōchō were linked sexually, though stated categorically by Saitō, is likewise unsupported by any evidence. But the Sōchō-Kitagawa-Jukei triangle does indeed merit scrutiny. See Saitō Sakae, "Sōchō," in Nakanishi Susumu et al., *Henreki,* vol. 9 of Nihon Aato Sentaa, ed., *Rekishi no gunzō* (Shūeisha, 1985), 201–45.

Whatever the nature of Sōchō's relationship with Jukei, her aristocratic heritage does appear to have led her to favor those of similar background. She was active in encouraging courtiers to come to Suruga from Kyoto; at least ten were to make the trip to the Imagawa domain during her lifetime.[89] Among those was Reizei Tamekazu, with whom Ujiteru studied *waka* for years.[90] She also encouraged marriage ties between the Nakamikado house and the Imagawa or their vassals. Her daughter became the wife of her nephew, Nakamikado Nobutsuna (grandson of Nobutane), and her niece married Asahina Yasuyoshi (see p. 135). Because of their mother, Ujiteru and Yoshimoto were themselves half courtier by ancestry. No other daimyo family showed that degree of inbreeding with the court. Jukei may well have relied on those with a similar Kyoto background for her cultural activities.

Jukei had considerable political acumen, and she was in turn advised by the monk Sessai (Taigen Sūfu, 1496–1555), who also exerted considerable influence on Ujiteru's successor, Yoshimoto (1519–60), during the greatest cultural efflorescence of the Imagawa capital.[91] Born into an important Imagawa vassal house, the Ihara, Sessai, as he came to be known, studied for eighteen years at Kenninji in Kyoto before being called back in 1522 to aid the young Yoshimoto, who was then still a monk with the name Baigaku Jōhō. Sessai stayed in Suruga until 1526—the exact years covered by the first book of *Sōchō shuki*—then returned to Kyoto, where for three years he frequently met the court literatus Konoe Hisamichi (1472–1544) and became well known for his skill at linked verse in Japanese and Chinese. Sanetaka knew Sessai as well. From 1529 to 1532, a period within which falls *Sōchō nikki* (1530–31), he was again in Suruga.

89. For a list of those aristocratic guests, see Owada, *Shizuokashi shi,* 1219–20.

90. For more on the relationship between Tamekazu and the Imagawa, see Semoto, "Reizei Tamekazu to Imagawa Ujiteru, Yoshimoto." Tamekazu's years in Suruga do not coincide with those covered in Sōchō's diaries, but Sōchō knew him personally and asked him for a verse in honor of the first anniversary of Ujichika's death, held on the twenty-third of the sixth month of 1527. See Yonehara, *Sengoku bushi to bungei no kenkyū,* 865.

91. On the relationship of Jukeini and Sessai, see Kurosawa Osamu, "Imagawake shikken Sessai Chōrō to Jukeini," in *Suruga no Imagawashi,* vol. 1, 73–85, and Owada Tetsuo, "Taigen Sūfu Sessai kenkyū," *Shinano* 29.5 (May 1977): 23–36.

When Yoshimoto was called back to secular life to succeed his elder brother, Ujiteru, on the latter's demise in 1536, Sessai continued to serve as his advisor and military strategist, while taking a leading role in the literary activity of the domain, often in the company of Reizei Tamekazu. He later crowned his career with an appointment to the abbacy of Myōshinji, a temple known for its "courtly atmosphere and deep political involvement."[92] With his Imagawa connections, his long experience in the noble houses of Kyoto, and his literary flair and political acumen, Sessai was perfectly matched to the courtly atmosphere actively fostered by Jukei. Though he was to become the *eminence grise* of the Imagawa house only on the accession of Yoshimoto, he was active in Suruga even in Ujichika's time and influential in Ujiteru's, his career beginning to flourish as Sōchō's neared its end. Sessai would later give instruction to the young Tokugawa Ieyasu, sent to Sunpu as a hostage from the Matsudaira of Mikawa to cement an alliance with Yoshimoto.

Sōchō never mentions Sessai in *Sōchō shuki* or *Sōchō nikki* despite the fact that Sessai was active in Suruga during those years. But there is evidence that Sōchō and Sessai were acquainted. At the request of Konoe Hisamichi, Sōchō compiled a primer on linking technique entitled *Renga tsukeyō* ("Techniques for Linking in *Renga*"), in which he included over two hundred *renga* verses he had composed between 1526 and 1528, together with judgments on them made by Sanetaka. The clean copy to be presented to the Konoe house was made by another *renga* master through the agency of Sessai.[93] A more telling example, though, of Sessai's new place at the heart of Imagawa cultural affairs even at the start of Ujiteru's rule is found in the postscript of the house history, *Imagawa kafu.* The document relates

92. Kurosawa, "Imagawake shikken Sessai Chōrō to Jukeini," 75.

93. *Renga tsukeyo* is included in Iwashita Noriyuki and Kishida Yoriko, "Honkoku Sōseki Kaishō to Sōchō shōkushū shūsei," in Ijichi Tetsuo, ed., *Chūsei bungaku: shiryō to ronkō* (Kasama Shobō, 1978), 464–79. The postscript of the work says only "Lord Konoe" (Konoedono). Yonehara theorizes that this is Hisamichi, probably because of Hisamichi's close association with Sessai (*Sengoku bushi to bungei no kenkyū*, 876). But Ijichi, in an early study of *Renga tsukeyo* and other works by Sōchō, assumes it refers instead to Hisamichi's son Taneie (1503–66) (Ijichi Tetsuo, "Sōchō no kushū *Kabekusa* sono ta ni tsuite no oboegaki," *Kokubungaku kenkyū* 7 (October 1952): 78.

that the biography of Ujichika was written after his death according to house tradition and that "the Reverend Taigen [Sessai] revised it at the request of the Dowager [Jukei]." Thereafter, the father of the anonymous writer of the postscript appealed to Ujiteru to ask Sōchō to simplify Sessai's composition.[94] It was thus Sessai who received Jukei's commission for the elegant *kanbun* version of the work. Sōchō became involved only later at the request of a third party.

It is unknown whether Sōchō's apparent lack of ties with Jukei and Sessai involved enmity. Advancing age probably played a role in Sōchō's declining activity, and it was natural that Sessai and not Sōchō should be commissioned to compose Ujichika's *kanbun* biography because of his greater skill in that medium. But it is likely that the characters and philosophies of Sōchō and Sessai were opposed. Sessai was the very model of the worldly Zen prelate, active in politics, partial to courtly tastes, and assiduous in the cultivation of those in power. Sōchō, by contrast, was through his entire life profoundly influenced by the thought and example of Ikkyū, a fiery and outspoken individualist who despised as hypocritical the secularity and display of the Zen institution of his day. Ikkyū reserved special hatred for his erstwhile fellow student Yōsō Sōi (1378–1458), who preceded him as abbot of Daitokuji and who embodied, according to Ikkyū, degenerate Zen practice. He expressed his hatred of the decadent practices of his day in bitter verses that included such lines as "Who of Linji's (Rinzai's) descendants correctly passes on his Zen properly?" and "There are no true masters, only false ones."[95]

Sōchō only knew Ikkyū for five years, more than two of which he was on the road with Sōgi. But for the rest of his life he was guided by Ikkyū's thought, and several times in *Sōchō shuki* he expressed his desire to die at Takigi, the last hermitage of the Daitokuji prelate. Sōchō's attitude toward worldly Zen priests was much the same as Ikkyū's, and he scathingly denounced them to his longtime friend Asahina Tokishige during their winter conversation of 1525:

> Where today can one find an inspirational teacher
> of the doctrines of "Separate Transmission Outside the Teach-

94. *Imagawa kafu*, 159–60.
95. These lines are taken from Ikkyū's anthology of his Chinese poetry, *Kyōunshū* (Shūon'an manuscript, nos.8, 169), in Nakamoto Tamaki, ed., *Kyōunshū, Kyōunshū shishū, Jikaishū*, vol. 5 of *Shinsen Nihon koten bunko* (Gendai Shichōsha, 1976).

> ings" and "Not Establishing Words"? Today's Zen practitioners are a pack of devils, of the lowest guttersnipe sort. Abbots, monks, and novices these days consort with the high and mighty, curry donations from provincial gentry, pursue their austerities only when it suits them, run hither and yon all day, and meet with other practitioners. But who are the masters they practice with themselves? Some say it is far better to meditate on the Holy Name.[96] I am more attracted to those who follow a simple and ignorant practice, as I do. (SS, 72)

Given Sōchō's attitude, it is hard to conceive of him having much in common with Sessai, who was at the same time assuming a role of increasing importance in the cultural life of the domain. That Sessai was a monk of the Myōshinji lineage, closely related to Daitokuji, made him an even more likely Yōsō to Sōchō's Ikkyū. Although there is no evidence linking Sessai and the criticism that plagued Sōchō during his last years, a closer relationship with Sessai and Jukei might have mitigated his trials. As Sōchō aged and his thoughts turned more to the hereafter and to the desire to die in Takigi or Daitokuji, he perhaps began to mentally distance himself further from the regime of Ujiteru, Jukei, and Sessai, with its increasing emphasis on court culture.[97]

Without additional information, then, Sōchō's relationship with Jukei and Sessai must remain entirely conjectural. But it would seem symbolic of the nature of the changing cultural alignment in Sunpu during Sōchō's last years that the house of his erstwhile supporter Lady Kitagawa should only five years following his demise be made into a temple, Rinzaiji, with Sessai as its first abbot, and that Sōchō's Yuan-period painting should pass after his death into Sessai's hands.[98]

96. That is, adherents of the Pure Land sects. Note that Ikkyū too professed at one point to have abandoned Zen for Pure Land beliefs. He wrote in his *Kyōunshū,* "In an earlier year I humbly received the portrait of the Zen priest Daitō Kokushi. Now I change my robes and join the Pure Land sect" (Nakamoto, *Kyōunshū,* 181).

97. Kishida Yoriko has pointed out how much of Book Two of *Sōchō shuki* is devoted to Sōchō's thoughts about his death, which had been prophesied for his seventy-ninth year (by the Japanese count). See Kishida Yoriko, "*Sōchō nikki* no kōsei," *Waseda Daigaku Daigakuin Bungaku Kenkyūka kiyō* 7 (1980): 61.

98. Yonehara, *Sengoku bushi to bungei no kenkyū,* 898.

It must be reiterated, though, that Sōchō continued, despite the cooler atmosphere in Suruga, to serve Ujiteru and deal with other Imagawa vassals as before. He suffered no irreconcilable break with his patrons, and his earlier services to the house were doubtless not forgotten.[99] But his travels to Atami and Odawara, in the domain of the Hōjō, may indicate a growing closeness instead to that house. It will be recalled that Lady Kitagawa was the younger sister of the founder of the Hōjō house, Sōun. Sōchō was also a longtime acquaintance of Sōun's son Ujitsuna (1486–1541), who succeeded as head of the Hōjō house in 1518.[100] Sōchō composed fifty votive *uta* for Mishima Shrine on Ujitsuna's behalf in 1525.[101] Neither Odawara, the site of Ujitsuna's castle, nor Atami figure in *Sōchō shuki* before the death of Ujichika, but each appears three times in his diaries thereafter, *Sōchō nikki* ending in Odawara on the thirteenth of the ninth month, 1531. Sōchō did, however, return thereafter to Suruga, and he died at Mariko on the sixth of the third month of the following year. Long in declining health, Sōchō took the waters of Atami for restorative reasons, but his interest in the Hōjō domain after the death of his old patron may not have been due solely to its hot springs.

Sōchō's career with the Imagawa provides in sum one detailed example of patronage in the Sengoku era. For most of his life, Sōchō enjoyed the advantages and security of the support of the Imagawa house and many of its vassals. But as this account has indicated, his life was one of continual periodic shifts between his Suruga protectors, other provincial domains, the Kyoto literary community, and Takigi and the Daitokuji network. Each satisfied for Sōchō different professional, artistic, and spiritual requirements.

99. Sōchō mentions in his diaries five meetings with Ujiteru for *wakiku* composition after the death of Ujichika, all on standard public occasions, and no *renga*. But a hundred-verse sequence with one link by Ujiteru, the *wakiku*, is preserved in Ijichi Tetsuo, ed., *Renga hyakuinshū* (Kyūko Shoin, 1975), 425–29, dating to the fourth year of Kyōroku, eleventh month, twenty-fifth day (early 1532). It is Sōchō's last extant hundred-verse sequence. By comparison, Reizei Tamekazu took part in more than fifty poetry sessions with Yoshimoto from 1536 to 1548 (the last statistic from Yonehara, *Sengoku bushi to bungei no kenkyū*, 866).

100. See n. 81 above.

101. This is *Ei gojisshu waka*, dated the twentieth day of the fifth month, 1525, a manuscript version of which is preserved in the Tenri Central Library.

In the case of the Imagawa, Sōchō, despite his priestly status, shared with Yoshitada, Ujichika, and Ujiteru the personal ties (*jōgi*) that characterized the traditional relationship between lord and vassal. As indicated earlier, his closest personal relationship of the three was with Yoshitada, and although he wrote that he was "in no special service" to him (*besshite miyazukai to wa nakute*; SS, 135), he added that he "was close to him day and night for years." Although Sōchō had yet to rise to prominence as a linked-verse poet when Yoshitada died, his ties to the house were firmly established during Yoshitada's lifetime.

By the time Sōchō returned to Suruga to serve Yoshitada's son in 1496, he was a professional *renga* poet of national standing and was in a position to provide a wide range of literary and extra-literary services to the domain. We have seen that these included the composition of votive *renga,* the direction of linked-verse sessions, tutelage in poetry and the classics, historical writing, the maintenance of contact with mutual acquaintances in Kyoto, acquisition of firsthand information from the provinces, and even negotiation with rival daimyo. In exchange for those services, Sōchō was assured of continual material support in a domain devoted to cultural pursuits and relatively free of the upheavals of Kyoto life. He continued to serve the Imagawa after Ujichika's death, particularly in the role of tutor to Ujiteru, but the number of meetings between the young heir and the octogenarian poet appear to have been relatively few, due partly no doubt to their disparity in age and to Sōchō's declining health, and possibly as well to factionalism within the Imagawa house.

The pattern of patronage just recapitulated differentiates Sōchō from the more typical *rengashi* model provided by Sōgi, Sōseki, and Sōboku, who had no similar long-term support. But if the latter poets did not enjoy such security, neither did they labor under the obligations that have been outlined in Sōchō's case. Sōgi and the others were likewise often required to compose poetry with, or lecture to, wealthy clients, with little room for personal choice. But they clearly had more autonomy than did Sōchō, who, as has been seen, more than once traveled at what amounted to a command from the Imagawa.

Imagawa patronage had both positive and negative effects on Sōchō's own literary output. Its most immediate benefit was that he could return to Suruga whenever he wished, sure of a place where he could reflect and write in comparative peace over extended periods.

Sōchō's whereabouts year by year are not entirely clear, but over a dozen of the extant diaries, handbooks, and verse anthologies by the poet that are roughly dateable appear to have been composed in full or in part in Suruga.

Moreover, Sunpu was one of the least provincial of provincial capitals, and Sōchō was assured of a convenient and relatively educated audience for his work. The Imagawa vassals, too, constituted a ready market for Sōchō's poetic expertise; they made up in literary energy and enthusiasm what they lacked in skill, and they provided the master with financial benefits and high regard.

But no matter how culturally progressive, Suruga was still far from the capital, the literary heart of the country. Except for occasional visits by other Kyoto poets or his own disciples, Sōchō lacked in Suruga the stimulation and competition of other gifted artists necessary for the creation of superior linked verse. It is significant in this respect that about three-quarters of Sōchō's extant linked-verse sequences made in or near Suruga are solo compositions (*dokugin*). Sōchō's diaries show that he frequently participated in sessions with other Suruga poets, but the fact that far more solo sequences survive suggests that his best work in Suruga was of necessity composed alone.

But even if the literary environment under the Imagawa was not of the caliber of that of the capital, Sōchō does not appear to have suffered serious constraints on his freedom to write how and what he pleased. To be sure, the historical chronicles he produced for the Imagawa are strongly biased in favor of his patrons. In addition, most of his extant poetry created for the Imagawa is highly formal in nature, consisting to a large extent of *waka* and *renga* for public occasions and of solemn votive works. But his honored literary position did not constrain him from including a wealth of unorthodox *uta* (*kyōka*) and *renga* (*haikai renga*) of a humorous and even bawdy nature in the diaries he undoubtedly expected his patrons would read. One need only consider the great circumspection Sōgi evinced in all his writings to appreciate the variety of tones and topics Sōchō showed in his, despite his position in Sunpu.

Regardless of the cultural advantages of the Imagawa domain, Sōchō nevertheless periodically felt the need for change. His life as a *renga* poet was to a great extent shaped by the dynamic created by his ties to the Imagawa on the one hand and by his personal artistic inclinations on the other. The long journeys through the provinces that punctuated his career were undertaken partly to make periodic contact with his widely dispersed acquaintances, to compose with them, and to disseminate the way of poetry, both through handbooks and personal example. But they were also directed toward refreshing his own poetic creativity and toward reestablishing his own artistic identity through visits to famous places and poetic sites or through other changes of scene and society. Sōchō, like Sōgi before him, was strongly attracted to the example of the wandering poet Saigyō (1118–90), and he viewed travel as a necessary part of poetic discipline (*shugyō*). The fact that Sōchō left Suruga so often despite its demands attests to the strength of that artistic motive. It was his poetic talent, combined with the thorough classical background he had acquired through years of study, that guaranteed him, as it had Sōgi, the means to survive outside the Imagawa purview when he so desired.

The provinces for Sōchō were thus not always cultural backwaters to be passed through; for the reasons just outlined they could also be ends in themselves, with a major role in his literary life. Some local poetry salons, such as that at Yamada in Ise Province, could be highly sophisticated.[102] But many of his journeys from Suruga were nevertheless undertaken with Kyoto as a primary destination. He had, as mentioned earlier, lived in the capital from about 1476 to 1496, excluding those times he was traveling. After his Kyoto cottage burned and he returned to Suruga at the end of those two decades, he was technically a transient whenever he returned to the capital, and *Sōchō shuki* shows him dividing his time between the Daitokuji network of temples and the residences of various acquaintances. He is nonetheless known to have traveled between Suruga and Kyoto at least eighteen times after returning in 1496 to the Imagawa domain.[103] It was in the imperial city and its environs that Sōchō could be sure of direct, high-level literary interaction with a wider range of literati and professional *rengashi* than he habitually met in Sunpu.

102. Arakida Moritake (1473–1549), composer of the famous *haikai* sequence *Moritake senku,* was one of the Ise poets who had dealings with Sōchō. For more on Sōchō's relationship with Ise poets, see *Nikonshū,* a record of discussions at Ise about *waka, renga,* and poetic lore, edited by Arakida Morihira and bearing a preface dated 1595 (Okuno Jun'ichi, ed., *Nikonshū,* Koten Bunko 335 [1974] and 343 [1975]).

103. Ōshima, "Sōchō nenpu."

Sōchō's ties to the Daitokuji network, on the other hand, were sustained less by poetry than by religious conviction. Zen for Sōchō was not a subsidiary pursuit to literature but a second pillar of his existence, and Ikkyū was as important an inspiration for him as Sōgi. The main reason for some of Sōchō's travels to the Asakura in Echizen Province was not for linked-verse composition but for donations to repair Ikkyū's Daitokuji, though he participated in poetry sessions on his visits as well. Takigi too was a minor artistic center itself, first under Ikkyū and then his disciples, and Sōchō's stays there involved poetic as well as spiritual communion, including a famous year-end *haikai renga* gathering in 1523 recorded in *Sōchō shuki* (SS, 30–34).[104] Like most other professional *rengashi,* Sōchō had taken holy orders and was therefore an *inja,* technically in retirement from the world. In his dedication to the teachings and example of Ikkyū, he showed far more commitment to the religious basis of the *inja* ethic than did many of his fellow professionals, who donned clerical robes for secular benefit.

Sōchō was a man of rich and varied parts, and his life and outlook were informed by the reciprocal influences and inherent contradictions of his concurrent careers as a servant (*kinju*) of the Imagawa, devotee of Ikkyū's Zen, and autonomous poet and man of letters. It is possible that this trifurcation of philosophy and purpose contributed to Sōchō's decision not to attempt to succeed Sōgi as doyen of professional linked-verse masters in the capital and as official Commissioner of *Renga* at Kitano Shrine. His relationship with the Imagawa and their vassals suggests both the advantages and the dangers of daimyo patronage in the Age of the Country at War.

104. See Nakamoto Tamaki, et al., "Chūsei shūkyō no kaitaiki ni tatsu Ikkyū," in the supplement (*bessatsu*) of Nakamoto, *Kyōunshū.*

Imagawa House Lineage

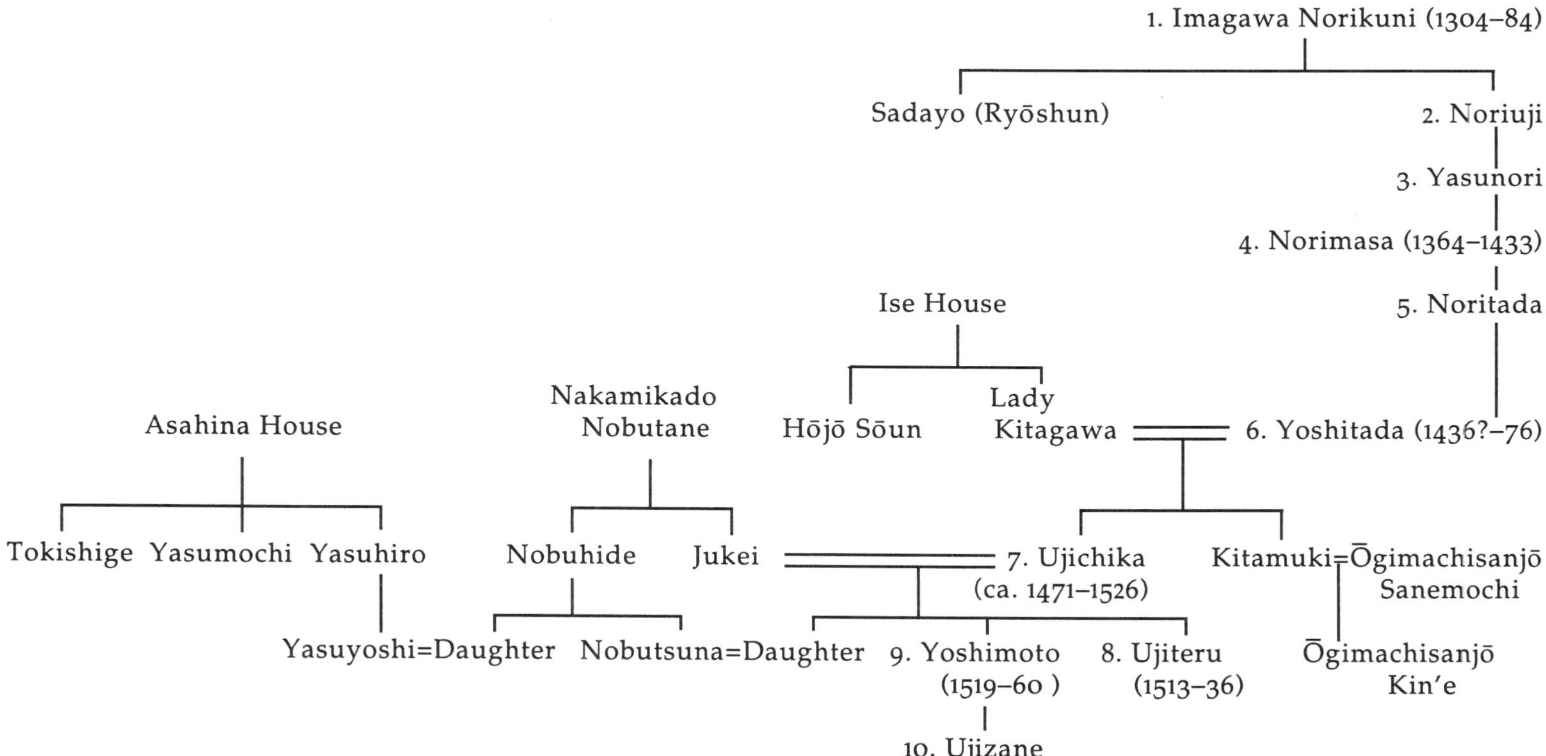

This chart is simplified; offspring are listed selectively and not necessarily in order of birth.

Index